USAIN BOLT
9.58

USAIN BOLT

MY STORY
9.58

BEING THE WORLD'S FASTEST MAN

WITH SHAUN CUSTIS

HarperSport

An Imprint of HarperCollins*Publishers*

First published in 2010 by
HarperSport
an imprint of HarperCollinsPublishers
77-85 Fulham Palace Road,
Hammersmith, London W6 8JB

www.harpercollins.co.uk

1 3 5 7 9 10 8 6 4 2

A catalogue record of this book is available from the
British Library

ISBN 978-0-00-737139-6

Exclusive photography Mark Guthrie
(www.MarkGuthrie.com)

Literary agents: NVA Management Ltd, Canary
Wharf Tower, 1 Canada Square, London E14 5DY (UK)
The Guma Agency (USA)

Printed and bound in Great Britain by Butler Tanner &
Dennis Ltd, Frome, Somerset

Usain Bolt was assisted in writing this book by British
journalist Shaun Custis. Shaun is a top sports writer with
the *Sun*, Britain's biggest selling daily newspaper, and a
former sports editor of the *Daily Express*. Shaun also wrote
Rio: My Story, the autobiography of Rio Ferdinand. He is
married with two children.

Mixed Sources
Product group from well-managed
forests and other controlled sources
www.fsc.org Cert no. SW-COC-001806
FSC © 1996 Forest Stewardship Council

FSC is a non-profit international organisation established
to promote the responsible management of the world's
forests. Products carrying the FSC label are independently
certified to assure consumers that they come from forests
that are managed to meet the social, economic and
ecological needs of present and future generations.

Find out more about HarperCollins and the environment at
www.harpercollins.co.uk/green

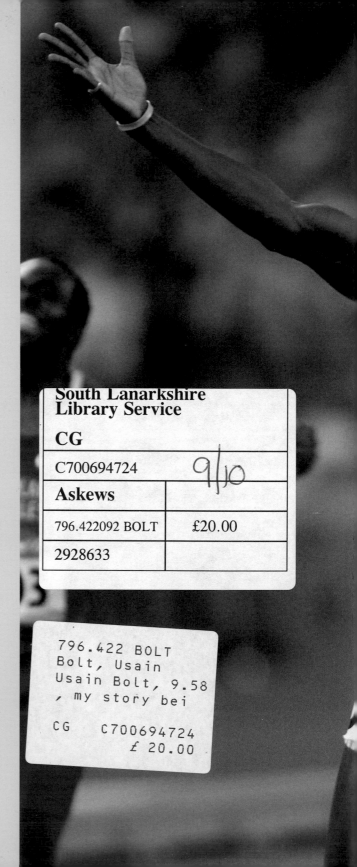

CONTENTS

THIS BOOK IS DEDICATED TO MY FAMILY
AND FRIENDS WHOSE ENCOURAGEMENT
CONTINUES TO KEEP ME GOING.

TO MY MOM AND DAD, I LOVE YOU!
THE VALUES I LEARNT FROM YOU ARE PRICELESS
—EXCELLENCE, PASSION, COMMITMENT,
DEDICATION AND HONESTY.

I AM ETERNALLY GRATEFUL.

CHAPTER 1

THE FASTEST MAN IN THE WORLD

USAIN BOLT – THE FASTEST MAN in the world. Never, ever do I get tired of hearing that. If you lined up a hundred people and asked them who the best basketball player in the world is, the best footballer, or the best cricketer, it is unlikely they would provide the same answer. But ask any of them, 'Who is the best sprinter in the world?' and there is only one answer – Usain Bolt. Why? Because that is what it says on the clock. There can be no dispute or argument. The record books say that over the 100 metres flat race, the true measure of human speed, I'm the fastest person that ever lived, completing the distance, as I did at the World Championships in Berlin, in 9.58 seconds.

It is said that the population of the earth is 6.8 billion and that approximately 107 billion have lived on this planet since man came into being. It doesn't get any cooler than knowing you are the fastest of them all.

I chose to be a sprinter, not only because I was the fastest kid in school, but also because I knew that politics couldn't interfere. In team sports it can be down to opinion whether you are the best. One coach might think you're good enough for his team, another might not, or the side could be picked on friendship or family ties. But in athletics you are either the fastest or you aren't – opinion doesn't come into it.

We had a grass track at the front of Waldensia Primary School, which is still there, exactly as it was, with a two-foot dip at the end of the straight, and when I first raced on it a guy called Ricardo Geddes would beat me. One day the sports coach, Devere Nugent, bet me a lunch that I could beat Ricardo. I like my food, so it was a big incentive. I won, enjoyed a nice meal, and never lost to Ricardo again. Winning that race was my first experience of the thrill of beating your closest rival, and from that day on my motto has always been 'Once I've beaten you, you won't beat me again.' There was quite a sporting rivalry between me and Ricardo, and I told him he should keep going with athletics but, like most kids in Jamaica, he wanted to play football, which he still does for one of the clubs on the island.

Much as I loved football and cricket, running came so easy to me. Once I got Ricardo out of the way, I was the fastest, not only in school, but in the whole parish of Trelawny. And, after a few years in high school when I put my mind to training, I was the quickest junior in Jamaica, then the world.

As I went on to win gold medals and set world records at the Olympics and World Championships, I felt exactly the same about taking on my Jamaican team-mate Asafa Powell and the Americans

"IT DOESN'T GET ANY COOLER THAN KNOWING YOU ARE THE FASTEST OF THEM ALL."

Wallace Spearmon and Tyson Gay as I did about racing against Ricardo Geddes. The aim was the same – to run as fast as you can and get to the line first, whether you are in the highly charged atmosphere of the 91,000-capacity Bird's Nest stadium in Beijing or on the school field.

Just like at school, I always try to go faster and faster. When I clocked 9.72 seconds to set the world 100m record in New York, I knew I could do better; when I ran 9.69 to win gold at the Olympics, I knew there was a lot more to come; and now, having run 9.58 in Berlin, I believe I can go even faster.

It is possible for me to run 9.4. You can't be sure when or where, but the major competitions are when I take it seriously and shine through. That's business time, and I'm not going to let anyone take my titles away, so the World Championships in Korea in 2011 or the London Olympics in 2012 are where it will probably happen.

To get from 9.58 to 9.4 will involve a lot of hard work – it will have to be the perfect race from the start, through the drive phase, to making sure my focus is straight ahead and maintaining my form to the end. I've never been the best starter, but it's improving, and I must stop looking from side to side, which is my worst habit. I lose time that way, but I can't help it. My coach Glen Mills says he could cure the problem in an instant by putting blinkers on me like they do with racehorses.

There is always something that could be better. Even when I think a race has gone well, Coach will say 'no' and take me back through it, pointing out the faults. If you run 9.58 you are entitled to think it all came together, but Coach tells me the drive phase out of the blocks was too short, I got too tight in the middle, and my head was all over the place, so there's room for improvement.

I do believe there is a limit to how fast the human body can run, though, and I don't see how the 100m record can ever go below 9.4. It is impossible to run 9.2, the body isn't made to go that fast, no matter how hard you train, how good a shape you're in or how good your technique.

As for the 200 metres, I don't know what the limit is. My 19.30 in Beijing broke Michael Johnson's record of 19.32, which had stood for 12 years. But I run the corner much more efficiently now, which is why I got the record down to 19.19 at the 2009 World Championships. I dream of being the first man to go under 19 seconds.

I was 24 in August 2010, and Coach says it will be at least two more years before I peak, maybe three. I'm nowhere near finished yet.

CHAPTER 2

HOME

THE FAMILY HOME

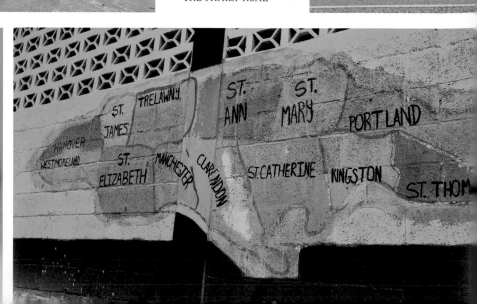

WHENEVER I GET STRESSED BY LIFE, Trelawny, the parish where I was born in north-west Jamaica, is where I return. It's quiet, with a slower pace to life. I can chill, and nobody bothers me. In Kingston, the Jamaican capital where I live because of my training demands, people are always calling up and coming to see me. That's good, but sometimes you need to get away from it all. In Trelawny I can sit on the veranda outside Mom and Dad's house, relax and clear my mind. People walk past and say 'hi' but that's it, man. They've known me since I was a youngster, so seeing me is no big deal.

I'm a normal human being who can get stressed out once in a while, not about track and field, which never worries me, but personal things like girls, business and stuff that needs organising. Back home I'll stay at Mom and Dad's in Coxeath near Sherwood Content, go round to Aunty Lilly's, visit my grandmother, and meet up with the guys who were my friends from way back when we played cricket together on the road outside our front door. We would cut a stump from a banana tree for a wicket and you were out if you hit the ball into the cow pen. We lost a lot of balls in there. The house has a light on the porch and we take a table out and play dominoes until the temperature drops so far that it's too cold to sit out any longer. Life doesn't get any simpler.

I'm still in touch with many of my old teachers from my very first school, Piedmont Basic School, as well as Waldensia Primary and William Knibb High School. I started Basic School when I was two, and one of the teachers, Mrs Sheron Seivwright, is still there. My Principal at Waldensia, Miss Mamrie Flash, who always looked out for me, helps out there, even though she has retired. My sports coach at William Knibb, Miss Lorna Thorpe, who was like a second mother, is still going strong too. I owe so much to all of them for bringing me up in the right way.

The drive home to Coxeath takes you off the main highway and away into the country along a winding single-track road, where somehow nobody crashes into anything coming the other way, even though there are so many blind corners and overhanging trees. Trust me, you get used to it. The journey takes you over a narrow bridge which crosses the Martha Brae River, where tourists who venture out that way can be seen drifting along on bamboo rafts. This is what they call Cockpit Country. It has all kinds of plant-life, insect and animal species and, at its heart, a tropical forest. On occasions when I had to go to work with Dad at the coffee company in Windsor I hated it, because it was deep into the vegetation and you'd get bitten by thousands of mosquitoes – they would never leave you alone.

The approach to home takes me past Piedmont and Waldensia and the little athletics track where it all started for me. It's a tight, 250m, not quite properly proportioned oval with an 80m flat track and that two-foot drop towards the finish line. I slipped once on the dirt on the corner during a house race at the age of nine and cried my eyes out. Whenever I look at that bend I can't help cussing.

As a child I was good at all sports, especially running, cricket and football. I liked being a goalkeeper and got loads of cuts and bruises from diving around on the stones in the grass making saves. Cricket was the big sport in primary school. I was a fast bowler as well as a number three batsmen. We were too young to use a proper cricket ball, but I was lethal with a plastic one and by grade six had learned to swing it through the air, which takes some doing.

My early school years were the best time for me, so carefree, but if you were naughty you would be disciplined. I was a bit of a prankster in school and would find myself being disciplined a few times. Dad would also stamp his authority at home when necessary, and I would run from him. He enjoyed the chase too. If I stepped out of line at anytime I would hear about it. I was lucky to have Mom and Dad in the same house – that has helped me to be balanced right now.

We actually had a lot of fun in school, like in grade five with Miss Roberts, who had false teeth which were always falling out. Once we went to a nearby sugar factory on a class field trip, and when we were

WITH MY FAMILY

giving her trouble she screamed at us so loudly that her teeth shot out of her mouth and fell down to the bottom of this hill. We couldn't stop laughing.

My best friend was 'NJ'. I was known as 'VJ', so it seemed natural to pal up with an NJ – full name Nugent Walker junior. I don't know why I was called VJ, but it's a Jamaican tradition that your parents and relatives call you by a pet name. If anyone calls me VJ rather than Usain you know they are from Trelawny – and if you think that's odd, my dad's name is Wellesley yet everybody calls him Gideon. Work that out.

The sports coach at Waldensia, Mr Nugent, who also took us for maths, was good, but he could be scary. One day he left us to study our 1-15 times tables – not something we were very excited about – so we started playing football round the classroom. Suddenly, as NJ was back-pedalling, Mr Nugent came from nowhere and grabbed him, hitting him twice and sending him out. I ran off so fast, thinking he was going to get me too, that I might have beaten 9.58 that very day. Mr Nugent wasn't really a beater, though, he was more of a pincher, having perfected a technique where he would nip you hard above the waist. That really hurt sometimes.

The first prize I won was a cup for a primary school race in grade four, and many more followed, although Mom had an amazing ability to break them as soon as I'd brought them home. There are a few still on display in the house, but I don't know how they've survived. Everyone in my family breaks things – glasses, tea-cups, plates. If it can be smashed, it gets smashed, so now they drink out of plastic cups and eat off plastic plates just to be on the safe side.

MY EARLY SCHOOL YEARS WERE THE BEST TIME FOR ME, SO CAREFREE, BUT IF YOU WERE NAUGHTY YOU WOULD BE DISCIPLINED.

I was picked for the parish primary school team after winning at Trelawny sports day and discovered that, while I might have been the fastest in my part of Jamaica, there were plenty of other guys on the island who could run too. In two years of competing at the national championships I was nowhere, which was hardly the mark of an athletics legend in the making. I got my ass kicked over 100 and 150 metres, but it didn't bother me because to me running was for fun, I wasn't practising for the Olympics.

However, I was quick enough to get a sports scholarship to William Knibb, one of the best schools in Trelawny. There was no other way I would have got in because, although I was reasonably bright, there were plenty of kids more intelligent than me. I could cope there – I wasn't a class dunce – but having earned my place on a sports ticket they expected me to be out training every night on the school field. For me this was all wrong – running was supposed to be a hobby, not something you had to work at – and I saw myself mainly as a cricketer who only did track and field because he was fast.

During my first year at William Knibb I skipped training after school all the time. I'd go into Falmouth with my friends Pete and Nimrod and we'd spend our dinner money on playing video games. We lived for going to the games room, which was run by a guy called Floyd. There were four Nintendo 64s and four TVs, and you paid a Jamaican dollar per minute to play, which we did until our money ran out. When I got home and my parents asked how training had gone, I would say, 'Yeah, it was good.'

They never suspected anything and I wasn't worried about being found out, but it all changed when one of my mom's nieces spilled on me and told my dad. He was not happy and came up to school for a meeting with the coach, Mr Pablo McNeil – who was a former Olympic sprinter – and the head of sports, Miss Thorpe. They lectured me, explaining the importance of training, that my athletics ability was

DAD

the reason the school accepted me and that if I didn't do it they would take the scholarship away. I understood, and I also knew Dad would kill me if I didn't do it – so, although I still went to the games room once in a while, training took priority from then on.

Mom and Dad were always at my races to cheer me on, but while my mom, Jennifer – or Jen-Jen to her friends – spoiled me and let me get away with things, Dad kept pushing to making sure I went to training, and the teachers knew they had his support if I was slacking off.

I didn't really start trying until grade nine, when I was about 14, but it was noticeable how my performances improved once I put in the extra effort. While I was the best runner in my school, there were guys from other schools, like Keith Spence from Cornwall College and another one called David from Emmanuel College, who used to beat me regularly. Yet once the effects of regular training kicked in they couldn't keep up, and the following year, 2002, I was winning the World Junior Championships. Training had helped, but I also realised I had talent, real raw talent.

The teachers at William Knibb deserve my grateful thanks for what I've achieved today, but I didn't always see it that way. They were so protective that they wouldn't let me join the school football team or do

football in PE in case I got injured, nor would they let me play cricket. When I went to the CARIFTA Games trials they deliberately put the school sports day on at the same time so that I couldn't take part in it with my friends. Then, the following year, when they realised I would be available to take part in it, they cancelled sports day completely.

I know that the head of sports, Miss Thorpe, had my best interests at heart. Whatever you wanted, you could always go to her. She even put up with me flicking her on the back of the ear whenever I walked past. She kind of got used to that.

One teacher, Mr De Souza, a football coach, was always checking on me. Whenever he saw me walking round without shoes on he would be screaming at me, telling me how important it was for a runner to keep his feet protected.

Mr Barnett, my athletics coach at school later on, was quite soft with me, but I produced the results for him. He didn't train me to extreme levels, because he realised that flogging me into the ground was not the way to get the best out of me. He was a funny man and would let me drive his Toyota Corolla on the main road once we got five minutes away from school, even though I didn't have a licence. I knew what I was doing, because Floyd from the games room had let me have a go in his car a few times. But my dad wouldn't teach me to drive and I still cuss him for it. He had two vans for work and a motor bike and never let me use any of them. Not once did he say, 'Come on, son, I'll show you.' With my height I could have been driving at the age of ten, but Dad was one for doing everything the right way. I had to have about 30 hours of lessons at driving school on Dad's orders. He was so strict and expected rules to be obeyed. You could never get round him.

MRS SHERON SEIVWRIGHT

PRINCIPAL, PIEDMONT BASIC SCHOOL

Usain was so full of energy when he entered school, earlier than most children. He came in at two years old, younger than the typical entry age of three and a half. His parents thought he was ready, and that he was. I've been teaching at Piedmont Basic School for nearly 25 years and remember Usain from the first day he started. Usain was always running around the classroom and impossible to catch even then.

He was tall for his age, which he obviously took from his dad, and a curious boy who asked lots of questions. He was interested in schoolwork as much as his sport and wanted to learn, but when I took Physical Education on Thursdays I could see he was a talented boy.

We have a checklist of everything children should know before they go on to primary school at the age of six. Usain scored good marks for everything, especially maths, and his handwriting was absolutely beautiful.

The whole school watched the Olympics on a big screen, and I was running around myself when he won. I put a scrapbook together of all his achievements for the children to look at, and the class are always interested in what he's doing.

We have a little song which goes, 'Children, children, do you know? Children, children do you know? Who is the fastest man on earth?' And, after a pause, they reply, 'To the World – Usain Bolt' and point to the sky together. It's special for them that the world's greatest athlete went to their school. When they are out on the field they all want to be as fast as him. I tell them the way to do it is to eat up, drink up and get strong. It's good to have a role model like that who children can relate to.

Along with The Digicel Foundation, Usain has helped with renovations to the school. The floor used to be just concrete, but they tiled it for us and decorated. They also put in cupboards and sinks and built a bathroom. When Usain comes to see his parents, he generally stops by to see us. Being famous hasn't changed him.

CHAPTER 3
FAMILY

MY HAPPY PERSONALITY AND LAID-BACK style which the public sees is not an act – it is exactly how I am away from athletics and comes from the way I was brought up. Mom and Dad would never go around cussing or arguing. Dad would talk and explain things, and you had to really push his buttons to get him angry. But if I didn't do what he said he would punish me to make sure I never did it again. Dad was big on discipline, and respect to him for that, because it's what made me the person I am today. It helped me understand life and he deserves thanks for that.

I didn't like being punished, of course not, and there where occasions when I felt it was totally unjustified, but it's what parents did. You didn't always know when it was coming either. Dad could take me by surprise, and when he grabbed me it was a case of 'Oh God, here we go'.

He was in charge of discipline in the house, while Mom spoiled me. I'm so like her, with the same type of hair, skin and even her laid-back style, while the only thing passed on from Dad was his height. He is a rules man who expects everyone to be on time. To make sure I was never late for school he would get me up at 5.30am, even though William Knibb – which was half-an-hour's drive away – started at 8am.

His view was that it was better to be an hour early than a minute late. He's late for nowhere. If he's in control of getting there, then he's not going to be late.

Dad didn't like us going out, he preferred us to stay in, and when we were younger we had to be home before he got back from work in Windsor, or else there was trouble. We had a dog called Brownie who served as a sort of early warning system – when you saw him running to the top of the hill to greet Dad, that was the signal to get inside.

Before getting home from school I would stop by at Aunty Lilly's, have a meal there and then have a second one with Mom and Dad. Aunty would be looking out for me from the veranda and knew just what I wanted – pork. Mom wouldn't cook pork, because she was a Seventh Day Adventist and her religion banned it. Jamaica is a very religious country which seems to have more churches than houses, and Mom spends a lot of her weekends in church. Strangely she would still cook me bacon and eggs for breakfast.

Aunty Lilly runs a shop and bar next to her house, and on Saturdays I would go there with Dad for sweets and ask her to 'make up', which meant asking for a bit of money to help me out. She was always good for it, and she still gives me yams from the farm she owns when I visit. While Dad chatted to Aunt Lilly and the locals, he would let me have a sip of beer, knowing that as soon as I drank it I'd fall asleep. I was so full of energy, this was the only way he could get any peace.

When I was younger I often stayed with my grandmother, Monica – now my only living grandparent. She lived in Reserve, about a 45-minute walk from our house, and in the summer holidays my cousin Charlene would be there too. Grandma is one of the best cooks ever, which was good because Mom doesn't like to cook. I joked with Mom about her not being able to cook very well. Grandma's corn-meal porridge was unbelievable. Even when it was ice cold it tasted good. Grandma still bakes me the most wonderful sweet raisin pudding when I go to the country.

Grandma, who is my mom's mother, was there for all of us. Everyone goes to her if they have a problem, which is probably why she's one of life's worriers. When I'm driving from Kingston to the country, which can take three and a half hours along dark winding roads, she prays the whole time, and I have to ring her the minute I get there. I forgot to do it once, because I was tired and went straight to bed, and when she rang the next morning to check if I was OK, oh my God, it wasn't a pretty conversation.

She's lived alone since Grandad died when I was nine – in an accident which happened right in front of me. He was on his way through the kitchen to get wood for the fire and slipped on the wet dirt floor, banging his head as he landed. He didn't move, and I went to the next house to get help, but there was nothing they could do for him. He had suffered a heart attack.

It was a terrible time for our family but didn't mean much to me because I was so young. When we went to the funeral my mom and her sisters were crying, but I didn't. I stood around at the graveside watching him being buried, then went off to play. You don't understand what death is at that age.

We would go to my other grandfather's in Windsor on a Sunday, which was a special treat for one big reason – he used to give us fresh cow's milk. Every time one of the cows had a calf, there was a three-week period where the calf would be drinking from the mother, and then after that we could have some. I would have a huge, five-litre pot of cow's milk and it was the best taste ever. It comes straight from the cow, then you boil it, skim it off and drink it hot. I can taste it just thinking about it. You haven't tasted anything till you've tried that, I promise you, and I looked forward to it so much. You couldn't drink five litres of cow's milk every day, but every week, fantastic. Neither he nor my grandma is with us any more, but I have such good memories of those times.

We lived slightly inland, so rather than spend our time by the sea

we would play for hours down by the river. I almost drowned once. There were some concrete slabs in the water and we would swim from one to the other, but one time we were having a backstroke race and I misjudged where I was. When I went to stand up where I thought the concrete deck was, there was nothing. It was the weirdest sensation as I quickly sank and began to freak out as water rushed into my mouth and up my nose. Fortunately I'd watched a programme only the week before which said that if you think you're drowning, the worst thing you can do is panic. Somehow I remembered it and managed to stop trying to breathe, went right down to the bottom, pushed off and came back to the surface. I can't describe the relief as I gulped in the fresh air. Who knows what would have happened if I hadn't seen that TV programme.

I didn't go back to the river for a good two months after that and have been wary of water ever since. I might fool around in the swimming pool at my house or splash around on the beach, but that's about it.

My brother, sister and I all have different mums, which is not unusual in Jamaica. Back in the days when Dad was growing up it was like that in a lot of families. My sister, Christine, is four years older than me and lived with us at various different times, while my brother Sadiki is eight months younger and would stay with us in the school holidays. Although my sister and brother are from different parents my mom always welcomes them to our home whenever they wish to visit. When Christine and I were growing up we didn't get along. Dad didn't like it when we went out in the yard to play football, and my sister used to tell on us for that and lots of other things. As you can imagine, I wasn't pleased with my sister for ratting me out, so we didn't get along well, but our relationship is a lot better now we're older.

To people in more well-developed countries it might seem we had a basic existence in our little two-bedroom rented house. We didn't

AUNTY LILLY

MOM & GRANDMA

" WHEN I STARTED MAKING DECENT MONEY AS AN ATHLETE IT WASN'T FOR ME IT WAS FOR MY PARENTS "

have much money but we never felt deprived. Dad had his job with the coffee company and said that if you worked hard you would always survive without having to beg from anyone. If we needed something he made sure we had it, but if he thought it wasn't essential then we probably wouldn't get it.

Amazingly, Dad actually decided that buying me a games console was essential because he and Mom were sick of me going off to the games room in Falmouth. He thought if I had the games at home they could keep a better check on me. When you had a Nintendo everybody came round to your house, especially if you had a new game. The house would be packed, with maybe ten guys in my room, but Dad accepted it because at least he knew where I was.

When I started making decent money as an athlete it wasn't for me it was for my parents. They have never lived a grand life and didn't want to move to some flash place away from the community so I've helped them to extend their house and build a garden. My dad is weird, he doesn't like to ask for anything and prefers to work for his money. Mom will ask but that might only be for the bus fare back to Trelawny from Kingston.

Long before I was famous they were both well known in the community, and would help anyone out. Dad always had a 'good morning' and a 'good afternoon' for everyone, which is how I learned to be well-mannered and polite. He still works in the grocery shop he opened after taking redundancy from the coffee company and it keeps him at the centre of local life. He will never stop working.

While I respect Dad I never felt he got the balance right between discipline and fun. If I wanted to go out he would set ridiculous curfews – as early as 10 o'clock at night, which was when all the parties were starting and gave you no time to impress the girls.

Despite that I did have a few girlfriends. The first was Kimlin Matteson, who went to William Knibb like me but didn't live nearby.

When it came to school holidays there was no way of getting in touch, because we didn't have telephones in the house or cell phones. After Kimlin I went out with Nakeisha Neal from the year above, but we split when I was 17 and moved to Kingston to be a full-time athlete. It was there I met Mizicann Evans, and we had a good time together for nearly seven years. She was the only person I've ever argued with, probably because we got on each other's nerves after so long together. Sadly, we broke up but still see each other sometimes because she's good friends with Mom.

There were two parties to go to at my school each year, but by the time I got there it was time to come home. So once I decided to party on and face the consequences from Dad for being late. I even got into trouble with him in front of my school mates when I was nearly 17.

It all started when I was sitting on a chair outside watching a class football match and some of my friends, who were messing about, sat in front of me and refused to move. There were some shoes beside me, which I threw at them, and when they threw them back at me they missed. A bunch of guys standing on a hill behind took one of the shoes, flung it and it hit this girl. Another girl then picked up the shoe and pulled it till she tore it.

The Principal said I had to get the shoe fixed. I refused, because it wasn't my fault, but I'd just got my first cell phone and Mom called to say the school had contacted Dad and he was going to come and sort it all out. If Dad was on his way it was very bad news, so I went off to Falmouth to get the shoe fixed and had to ask my Aunty Annette for money for the repair because I didn't have enough. I got the job done, raced back to school and returned the shoe to the kid who owned it.

Everything was good, or so I thought, until I walked past the staffroom door, took a glance and saw my dad was in there. Worse still, he saw me. It was not good after all. Dad called out 'BOLT!!!" in the loudest voice and grabbed hold of me. You can imagine the trouble I was in after that.

NORMAN PEART

MANAGER

Following my short stint as an athlete, where I competed in the 800 metres through high school, I was not sure what my next step would be, but things changed dramatically when I became manager for this young phenomenal star, Usain Bolt. In February 2002 my life made a 360-degree turn and has not been the same since. Now I can look back and say, 'I have the template of how to manage a star athlete.'

I am a graduate of William Knibb High School, like Usain, but lost touch with the school's track programme, so I had not heard about Usain before I started mentoring him. I was working with the tax office in St James (Montego Bay) when Principal Margaret Lee rang to ask me to assist with the school's track and field programme. That was to be quite a challenge as I left work at 5pm – by the time I had driven over to the school, training would be done. The Principal called back and said there was a special athlete she wanted me to consider.

I met Usain for the first time on a Friday afternoon, introduced by Alton McDonald, a PE teacher who was at the school when I was a student. When I enquired about Usain I was told he was obedient and talented, two great attributes I looked for in people generally. Of course I would later learn that Usain could be as stubborn as any regular teenager was.

I knew that his parents would be a vital piece of the puzzle I was to put together; but my meeting with them went smoothly. I realised they had a handle on him, and that led me to take on Usain as a project. His dad stood out as the main disciplinarian, with support from his mum. I liked that.

I got the opportunity to see him perform at a regional track meet in Montego Bay, where he ran a leg on 4x100 and 4x200m relays, and he was fantastic in both. The rush of adrenaline was fast ... and I thought, 'Do I have an Olympic champion on my hands?'

In July 2002, at the World Junior Championships in Kingston, Usain took the world by storm with his spectacular win in the 200 metres, beating Brendan Christian (Antigua) and Wes Felix (USA). The spotlight was now on, and I realised my work was going to be more challenging.

I was not trained to teach, but I knew what it would take to make Usain successful, and I took the bull by the horns. Usain claims he resented me initially, but he was way too polite to show that. He did make a few mistakes, but he was generally cooperative.

In the high school championships in 2003, Usain upset the favourite in the 400 metres, Jermaine Gonzales, and won the 200 metres. In fact, his 200m time of 20.25 seconds was the third fastest in the world at any level. I then went to the parents for a much more serious talk. With one more year left in school, we knew his life was at a critical juncture. He was completing high school that year, but had the opportunity to come back, as he had two more years' eligibility for the national athletics championships.

With the vision of Usain becoming a star within five years, at the Beijing Olympics, proper staffing to enhance his career was essential. With new coach Fitz Coleman and an endorsement contract from Puma secured, a very good competition agent was required. Through a strong recommendation from Juliet Campbell, a private meeting at a Paris restaurant in 2003 with PACE Sports Management (formerly KIM Sports Management) started the process.

There I met Tom Ratcliffe (American), Ricky Simms (Irish) and Marion Steininger (German). The meeting went well but of course Usain was not competing until next season so there was no need for a quick decision. It was actually sometime in early 2004 that the contract was hammered out with Tom Ratcliffe. Tom left the company to do his own agency so Ricky became the point man. PACE is still Usain's agency and I must say a job well done to this date.

When I was transferred to the Constant Spring tax office in Kingston, Usain moved in with me.

Over an 18-month period with two tutors and me, Usain was successful in five subjects, giving him the minimum qualification for college. So we had that in the bag. College, however, was put on hold, as he spent only one semester at the University of Technology (UTech).

Disappointment came in 2004, as injury prevented him from defending his world junior title. He qualified to compete at the Olympic Games in Athens, but did not go past the first round.

Decision time again ... and after consultation with Usain we decided it was time for a new coach. On our return from Greece, Usain approached Glen Mills. We completed those negotiations.

The 2005 World Championships in Helsinki now became a test of the capabilities of Coach Mills. Usain reached the 200 metres final, but pulled up with an injury and walked to the finish line. The supporters were not complimentary. There were comments about his extracurricular activities, including clubbing, and things got a little out of hand. We kept to the plan ... he missed the 2006 Commonwealth Games and the criticisms intensified.

We again stuck to the plan ... things changed in 2007, and again international attention grew. With two silver medals, in the 200 metres and the 4x100m relay, there was some backing off. In the meantime the business of track and field was being pursued.

I then figured that if Usain was not winning, our negotiating tactics were worthless. Puma and Digicel were still our strongest supporters.

Before Beijing we knew we were on to something, but then, 9.69 seconds later, all our lives changed... That spectacular performance in the 100 metres created such a stir that the number of requests I have received went beyond unbelievable.

The learning curve has been steep, but a team has been put in place to support the star we have on hand. Usain's incredible performances are in keeping with the brands he has been associated with, and the team around him complements his achievements.

The experience of managing an athlete of Usain's calibre has changed my life in several ways. All of us have been affected, in a positive way ... creating far more opportunities than I could ever dream of.

WITH RICKY AND
MARION FROM PACE

CHAPTER 4
GETTING STARTED

MY COACHES IN THE EARLIER PART of my career included Olympian Pablo McNeil, Bobby Brown, Darland Clarke and Christopher Mitchell. It was not uncommon for young, upcoming stars in rural Jamaica to have so many coaches. The experience was interesting.

The great advantage of being a young runner was being able to travel to different places with your friends. It was like going on your holidays. One of the biggest events for high school kids was the Penn Relays, which were held at the University of Pennsylvania in the United States. The competition has a history going back over

100 years, and the university is credited as the birthplace of relay racing. To fly over and take part in a competition which attracted teams from all over the world in front of thousands of spectators was a real thrill. They say more athletes have run at the Penn Relays than in any other athletics event, Olympics included. We never won there, but it got me dreaming about what it would be like to take part in a major championships.

As my new training regime at William Knibb took effect I won a silver medal in the 200 metres at the Jamaican High School Championships and silvers in the under-17s competition at the 2001 CARIFTA Games in Barbados over 200 and 400 metres. When the CARIFTA Games were held in Bahamas in March the following year, I turned the silvers into golds and set championship records in both events.

It was that time in Nassau that I was first christened the Lightning Bolt. I'd already been called the Thunder Bolt by the regional media and my friends would joke about it. But this was far better. Lightning Bolt had a real sense of excitement about it – a flash and you were gone. As I crossed the line in the 200 metres, the crowd chanted 'Lightning Bolt, Lightning Bolt,' and it got louder and louder. It was very cool.

Six years later when I set the world 100m record, running 9.72 in New York, they loved the name Lightning Bolt, because there had been thunder rumbling and lightning cracking around the Icahn Stadium before the race. One of the American commentators claimed to have invented it that night but, I'm sorry to disappoint him, he didn't – it was the crowd in Nassau, long before he got on the microphone.

I was still only 15 at the 2002 World Junior Championships which, as luck would have it, were held in Kingston. The competition was for under-20s, which made me much younger than many of the other athletes but, being almost 6ft 5ins tall, I didn't look out of place and certainly didn't look 15.

It is the one and only time I've felt real pressure. There was a lot of attention on me and a girl sprinter called Anneisha McLaughlin, and we were being talked of as the stars of the future. There might have been even more pressure on Anneisha, who had taken a silver in the relay at the previous world juniors and a bronze in the 400m at the world youths.

There was a list showing the fastest times in the world that year, on which I was placed fifth, but none of the four above me showed up in Kingston. That meant I was in with a real chance of victory in front of my home crowd. In later years I would be disappointed if my main rivals weren't present, because it was important to show I could beat everybody, but back then the less challengers the better as far as I was concerned.

Having got through to the 200m final, I was extremely nervous walking out through the tunnel into our national stadium. The crowd were cheering, and I thought it was all for Anneisha, who had gone out ahead of me. Then, as I set foot on the track, the place went ballistic with shouts of 'Bolt, Bolt, Bolt.' I was a kid of 15 and the enormity of it hit me. I cannot recall feeling so much pressure in my life. I had never been in a situation like this before.

I was so messed up that I put my spikes on the wrong feet, left on right and right on left. My hands were shaking. When I finally got the shoes on the correct feet it was almost impossible to stride out and do my warm-up sprints, my body was so lacking in energy. It was going to be a disaster.

As we went to the blocks I wasn't feeling good at all. When the starter announced 'On your marks, set...' and then the gun went off, I was last off the blocks, my arms so weak I barely got going. It is hard to explain how tense I felt. No race I've ever been in since compares. Everything appeared to be in slow motion, but as I started to run the tension drained away. I rounded the corner and the crowd gave me

a tremendous push as they cheered me on down the home straight. I came right through the middle of the other sprinters, hit the front and finished four metres clear of the rest.

The place went absolutely crazy. I hadn't thought of doing the sign of a bolt being fired in those days, so I saluted the spectators military style, and they did the same back. Ever since that day I've joked around with the crowd and come up with something to involve them in my victories. The interaction we have gives me a buzz, and the spectators have become an important part of the Usain Bolt show.

It took a while getting round the track to see my parents, who were sat in the grandstand. When I can't see them at my events they only have to shout 'VJ!' and I can find them, because everybody else

is shouting Usain. It was the same later at the Olympics. They were so pleased for me. I recognised how much they'd done to help me, it was a victory for us all. There were hundreds of autographs to sign, with people falling over each other offering their congratulations.

For the first time I had big press coverage in Jamaica – I was on the front and back pages of the papers. It now feels as if my name has been in the news every day since, whether I'm racing or not. Suddenly everything about me was news. When I got an eye infection called conjunctivitis, which Jamaicans call 'pink-eye', even that made the paper – which would have been a real eye-opener, if I could have opened my eye.

I was proud of what I'd achieved. To win an individual medal for my country was a big moment. I've been representing Jamaica since the age of 14 and I'm very patriotic, I love my country and the people.

I'VE BEEN REPRESENTING JAMAICA SINCE THE AGE OF 14 AND I'M VERY PATRIOTIC

Meanwhile my schoolwork had started to slide in the build-up to the world juniors. I was more focused on track and field, and the Principal, Mrs Margaret Lee, decided I needed a mentor to watch over me, so I could train as much as required but also get my schoolwork done in the evenings. I didn't agree with the idea, which as far as I could see just meant more school. Now there would be another person telling me what to do apart from my dad and the teachers. But my parents thought it was the right thing to do, so there was no choice in the matter, and with that Mr Norman Peart came into my life.

Mr Peart was a former pupil at William Knibb who had been a good high school runner and understood the demands on a young athlete. He worked in the tax office in Montego Bay and would come to my house two or three evenings a week to help with my studies and sometimes pick me up after training. At first I resented him being around, spoiling my fun, but I gradually got used to it. When I later left William Knibb to join the High Performance Centre in Kingston, where they develop track and field athletes, Mr Peart got his job transferred and came too. Now he is my full-time manager. The work we put in together with the tutoring helped me pass five subjects at the CXC level.

The year after winning the world juniors I became the world youth 200m champion in Canada. It was not unexpected, as it was only for sprinters aged up to 18, which made it easier than the juniors. I remember the competition more for the laughs with my friends Andre Willington and Spoony than for the races.

There was no question of me losing, so the night before the final I worked on a special breakdance routine in front of the mirror until I got it perfect. Andre and Spoony thought it was really cool, winding me up to make it better and better. They told me how they were going to be in the stands and it had to be good to impress them.

As soon as I won I ran to where they were supposed to be and prepared for my brilliant breakdance. They weren't there. Where the hell were they? There was no point doing the dance without them, and rather than enjoy the victory I cussed them for ages when I got back to where we were staying. I said I'd practised all night to get it right and was so angry. They couldn't stop laughing and admitted they'd forgotten about it and went off shopping at the mall instead.

I was supposed to run the 400m at the youths as well but didn't want to – it would have got in the way of our fun. If you are entered for an event, you have to give a reason why you can't run, so there was nothing else for it, I had to fake a bout of diarrhoea. When the doctor heard about my 'problem' he sent me to the bathroom where I had to sit for ages to convince him. Luckily nobody actually came in to check the evidence, though – they took my word for it.

In the Jamaican High School Championships of 2003 I broke both the 200m and 400m records by a good margin. It was clearly time for a serious discussion about whether athletics should become my full-time career. If that was the case there was no reason for staying at

WITH CAROLE
BECKFORD AND
MR PEART

William Knibb any longer, and after a meeting between my parents, my teachers and Mr Peart, I joined the big world, moved to Kingston, and became a professional athlete.

I signed my first contract with the Puma sports company, a four-year agreement. It seemed like an enormous sum of money. Puma was the sponsor of the Jamaican team for all major events. The company is ingrained in the country, and they've been very good to me. Because of my success William Knibb is sponsored by them and the school never has to buy any athletics kit for the pupils, it is all provided.

I'd never had any sort of job, not even a part-time one, and now I was being paid to run. When I look back, though, Puma got me on the cheap, given that I was the best junior in the world, and I still joke with Mr Peart that he should take the blame for that. He was the man with the business degree. But we were both learning together and we are a lot wiser today.

On moving to Kingston Mr Peart and I stayed with another athlete who has become a good friend, Jermaine Gonzales. Then Mr Peart got married and I moved in with him and his wife. He would go off to work at the tax office during the day, but was also my manager, responsible

for organising my life. I needed him around because my parents weren't there. Like my dad, he wasn't keen on me going out and kept teaching me life lessons about how, if I wanted to be a great athlete, I shouldn't go off drinking and clubbing every night of the week. For a red-blooded teenager who had moved from the country to a bustling city there were a lot of attractions and distractions, but Mr Peart, unlike my dad, let me find out the good and the bad for myself and never stopped me going anywhere.

Early in 2004 I broke the world junior record for 200 metres at the CARIFTA Games in Bermuda, running 19.93. For four months until the Athens Olympics it was the fastest time in the world by anyone, in the juniors or seniors. On the face of it, being a full-time athlete was working, but I wasn't happy. I didn't like the training regime imposed by my new coach Fitz Coleman.

HE SAID I WASN'T A SCHOOLBOY ANY MORE, THAT THIS WAS PROFESSIONAL ATHLETICS, AND TO LEARN TO TOUGH IT OUT

At high school a standard training session consisted of around five 300m runs which were not flat out. When I got to Kingston it was about doing weights all the time and hard 700m, 600m and 500m runs. It was too much work in my estimation, and I told Mr Coleman my body couldn't cope. He would just say I should do it, but I told my parents and Mr Peart that I couldn't. Mr Peart was on Coach's side. He said I wasn't a schoolboy any more, that this was professional athletics, and to learn to tough it out. It wasn't the way to get the best from me. I warned them that if I got injured they would all be to blame.

MISS MAMRIE FLASH

PRINCIPAL, WALDENSIA PRIMARY SCHOOL

Usain's current fame has put the school in the spotlight. Television crews from all over the world have come ... from Britain, Germany, Finland, Switzerland and Mexico, and journalists from *Time Magazine* in America. The children have got quite used to it.

When Usain won the Olympics, I cried, I couldn't help it. I was at a principals' conference watching the 100 metres on television and was completely overcome. This was the same Usain who was such a joy to teach – friendly, happy, well-mannered, and full of energy.

When he came back from the Olympics we went to a celebration at the stadium and were all given commemorative T-shirts. Then we went to William Knibb High School for another ceremony, where Usain presented us with a big bag of cricket gear and a large refrigerator, which we just about managed to load on to the bus.

Usain was a reasonably bright child, in the top ten of the 40 students in his class. His parents made sure he always did his homework, and his mother was president of the Parent Teachers' Association (PTA). She helped to raise funds for us through concerts and barbecues.

From early on we knew Usain was going to be a fierce competitor. His main contender at the school in running was a much shorter Ricardo Geddes. They used to be so competitive with each other, running around the track outside the front of the school. Our school sports day is still held on that same track, and all the kids want to be like Usain.

I wasn't around the last time he visited, and he phoned just to tell me he hadn't forgotten me. No wonder we think he's special.

CHAPTER 5
NEW
COACH

I HAVE A CONDITION CALLED SCOLIOSIS, which causes my spine to curve to the right and has made my right leg half an inch shorter than the left. However, this wasn't discovered until after Athens, when I'd split from Mr Coleman and went to train with Glen Mills, who advised me to get a proper check-up.

A doctor carried out a detailed examination, diagnosed scoliosis and thought I was such a mess I might have to give up athletics altogether. I was seriously worried, but I then went to see a German surgeon called Hans Müller-Wohlfahrt, who is famous for treating top footballers, and he assured me he could put me right. He has been as good as his word.

Until that breakthrough I'd just got on with training, struggling with my sore back and doing what I was told. When I broke the world junior record, everyone thought Mr Coleman's regime had been proved right, but I was concerned about a lack of speed work in my training programme, and it was no surprise to me when I pulled my hamstring as we were preparing for the Olympics. I knew it was all related to my back problems.

Mr Coleman was determined I should go to the Olympics, hamstring troubles or not, and we worked and worked to try and get me fit. But then I picked up an Achilles tendon injury in training when turning to avoid another athlete who had stepped across me. It wasn't serious, but it set me back again.

I wasn't bothered about going to the 2004 Olympics. It was too early for me, too soon in my development, and I wasn't going to win based on how unprepared I was. My preference had been to do the world juniors in Italy and defend my 200m title. It annoyed me that the guy who went on to win the juniors in my absence, an American-born athlete representing Italy called Andrew Howe, who is now a long jumper, had talked about how much he wanted to run against me and what he was going to do to me, blah, blah. He ran 20.28 to win and I was like 'please' – I was running 19.93.

The Olympics should have been an occasion to look forward to. It is a significant moment in any athlete's career, but given my poor condition I couldn't think about enjoying it. I'd talked to the coach, my parents and Mr Peart and told them my workload was too much, that I was being pushed too hard, but nobody was listening.

Coming out for my 200m heat in Athens I knew it was a complete waste of time being there. I didn't have the heart for it. I could have got into the first four and reached the next round but I wasn't interested. I was in fifth place approaching the finish and could have got past the athlete ahead of me but didn't bother. It didn't make any sense. Even if I'd made it through, I was never going to be able to do anything and go further. I wanted to get out of Greece, which had been a very bad experience for me.

I returned to Jamaica deflated and into a wall of criticism from the public, who had been expecting great things. I explained about my injury, but in Jamaica they don't understand or care about excuses. The feeling was that if I was injured I shouldn't have gone to the Olympics. They were cussing me and looking for other reasons for my failure. The talk was that I was going out too much and wasn't dedicated enough.

The reaction got me down for a while, but it taught me that the most important thing is to go out there and do it for yourself, and not to worry about pleasing other people. If you win they will be happy and if you fail they won't. It's as straightforward as that.

My relationship with Mr Coleman wasn't helping. It was not good; he didn't understand me. I had heard good things about Glen Mills, who was a coach to the Jamaican team and also trained athletes at the High Performance Centre. He was more of a sprinters' coach than Mr Coleman, and the other guys were doing well with him, so I asked Mr Mills to take me on, then left it to Mr Peart to negotiate.

Glen Mills had coached many top athletes, including the 2003 world 100m champion Kim Collins, and was so different to all my previous coaches. He discussed things with his athletes and worked with them. He didn't just tell you what to do like a teacher in class.

He began by trying to find out the reasons for my many injuries and sent me to various doctors, until one discovered the scoliosis and said it explained my hamstring problems. It was a relief to find out, and although it was suggested I should give up athletics, me and Coach saw things differently. We took it as a positive, because at last we knew what we were dealing with and could plan training accordingly.

I soon came to trust Mr Mills completely. If I told him I couldn't do something or didn't think an aspect of training suited me, he would talk to me about it. If he then still decided he was right, he

would explain why and tell me to get on with it. That was fine by me. I had full confidence in him and that he was making the correct call. Turning out top athletes was Mr Mills's job, and he knew how to do it. He had a lot of experience from years of going to the Olympics and World Championships and knew what made winners and losers. He told me about the good athletes and the bad athletes, where they were strong, where they were weak and why.

While I do the mental and physical work, Coach fine-tunes me, like a mechanic with a top-of-the-range sports car. If you put a big turbo on a car but you still feel you should be getting more from it, you take it to the Dyno shop where they do a complete check and tweak little bits all over to get that bit more out of its performance. That is what Glen Mills does with me.

He understands that I'm lazy and that I might miss training. That's how I am. He doesn't get mad with me, he lets it go, but if I'm absent from more than one day's training he will be ringing me

asking what's up and why I've not been there. I respect him totally and if he says we need to buckle down, I will buckle down, even if that means no partying for a month. People who don't know him properly think he's grumpy, but we have a laugh together. He doesn't much like the media, though, and rarely gives interviews.

In 2005 I won the Central American and Caribbean Championships. They did not provide the strongest opposition, but the idea was not to go up against any stiff competition and stress the body out. The plan was to ease my way through to the World Championships in Helsinki. We weren't expecting me to make the 200m final in Finland, because of all my injury problems, and it was a surprise to get there at all. In the end I got cramp 60 metres from the line when challenging for the lead and hobbled over the finish line in about 26 seconds, a long way behind the winner Justin Gatlin. It had been pouring with rain, it was cold, and the start kept being delayed by one athlete who

was fiddling with his blocks, then couldn't get his feet right on the pressure censors. I'd never run in rain like it, and because of my injuries getting cramp was not such a shock.

Coach also said that by running the corner so hard and being so tight on my body it put a hell of a strain on my hamstring. We later discovered there was a small tear in the hamstring, which wasn't too serious, and I went back to Dr Müller-Wohlfahrt to get patched up.

Far from leaving me down-hearted, that final gave me a lot of

belief. I'd been up there with the leaders from the hardest lane, the one with the sharpest corner and which is especially difficult to run if you are as tall as I am. It is one of the reasons why in the heats you always want to be sure of being one of the fastest qualifiers, because that way you get a better draw in the middle lanes. I don't think I would have won, with the likes of the Americans Tyson Gay and Wallace Spearmon in the race too, but I would definitely have made the top six. It was very encouraging.

The following year, 2006, was not a big year in our programme. Coach thought it best not to go to Melbourne for the Commonwealth Games after I picked up a slight strain at the Gibson Relays in Kingston. Missing out on Melbourne didn't bother me. I believed in what we were doing and our long-term goal that it would all come together from 2007 onwards.

But Jamaicans were having serious doubts about me. They questioned why I hadn't made the progress they felt I should have done since winning the world juniors. Every year I'd started well then faded away, and it was said that I'd never make it to the very top of the sport. There were even claims I'd been paid to pull up at the World Championships because, according to some commentators, the way I stopped wasn't the way you should do it if you got cramp. Around the world most people understood that finely tuned athletes get injured, but not in Jamaica – you have to win whatever the circumstances.

As I saw it, I was young, time was on my side, and I had become more hardened to the criticism, having gone through it after the 2004 Olympics. I felt bad at letting people down but, whereas in the past my priorities had been about pleasing the public, they were now about putting myself first. If I was successful, the rest would fall into place. Coach explained that injuries were part of track and field, that they happened to everyone at some time in their lives, and what you've got to do is find out what caused them and move on.

I earned my first senior medal in September of 2006 – a bronze over 200 metres at the World Athletics Final in Germany behind Wallace Spearmon, who was second, and Tyson, who got gold. A week later I took silver at the IAAF World Cup in Athens, which Wallace won.

It was annoying the way Wallace was always fractionally ahead of me, and I wondered why. Coach had told me to learn to lose, because by doing so you could figure out what you needed to do to win. There was always a reason for losing, and I realised I was looking behind almost as soon as I started every race. This was slowing me down and costing vital time. So I said to myself one day that I would try not looking behind for as long as possible. I managed to do that until coming off the corner and, when I eventually did look back, I was clear. From that moment on, Wallace never beat me again.

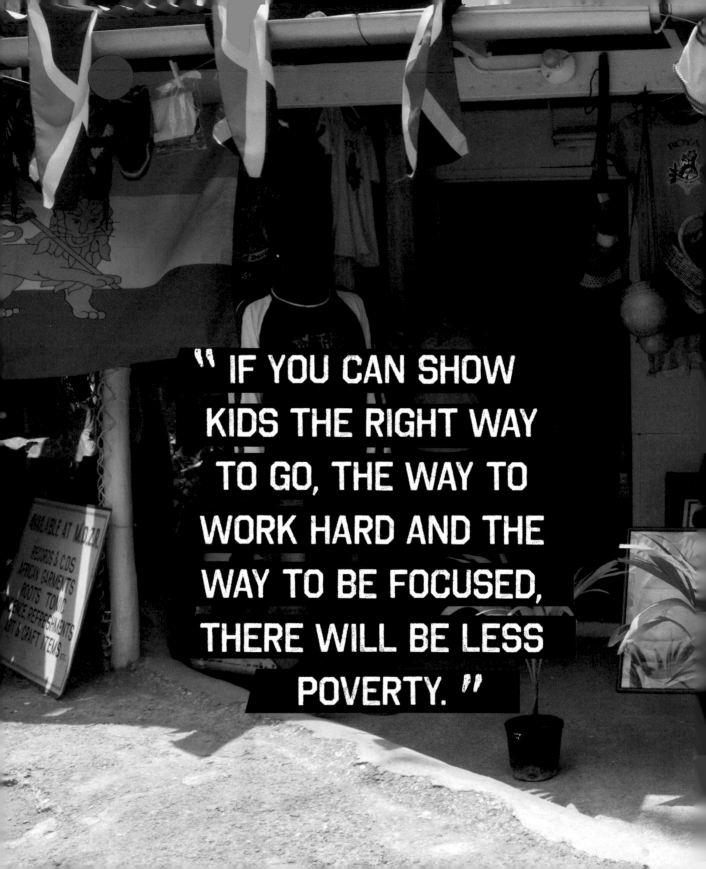

" IF YOU CAN SHOW KIDS THE RIGHT WAY TO GO, THE WAY TO WORK HARD AND THE WAY TO BE FOCUSED, THERE WILL BE LESS POVERTY. "

DEVERE NUGENT

**FORMER SPORTS TEACHER,
WALDENSIA PRIMARY SCHOOL**

'He's beginning to believe.' That's how I thought of Usain. He had begun to believe in his own ability, and in Beijing, China, he realised just what he was capable of.

I'm a pastor now with the Baptist Union, and I think God presents opportunities to us. We can either drop the ball or catch it. Usain has caught it very well indeed.

Usain was seven when I first saw him, and I immediately noticed the rivalry between him and Ricardo Geddes. Bolt would win over 150 metres, but Geddes could beat him over 60 metres until Usain eventually got the better of him.

I thought of Usain as more of a cricketer then than a sprinter. When he was in grade three, at the age of eight, he was playing with the 11-year-old boys in grade six. You couldn't tell the difference because of his height. He batted number three, was a good fast bowler and one of the best gully fielders I've ever seen. Any sport he decided to pursue he would have made it, football as well. He could play in goal or outfield.

His father, Gideon, and I had many conversations about his sporting ability and how best to develop it. In recognition of Usain's talent, he got a scholarship to attend William Knibb High School. I encouraged his father to send him to a school with a strong track and field programme. I knew he was intelligent enough to survive there. The school gave its complete support.

I continued passing on little tips for him through his father about what he should do in his races, and Gideon, Pablo McNeil, Dwight Barnett, Fitz Coleman, Glen Mills and myself have all helped him. What I discovered with Usain was that, if he respected you, he would give you 250 per cent.

That is why Glen Mills has been such a success with him. What coach Mills is getting from him now has always been in there. He could run 10.3 seconds for the 100 metres when he was 15, which is blisteringly fast for someone of that age, but it needed someone to take him to the next level.

I've watched all his big races on TV and YouTube. The Olympics and World Championships were absolutely awesome. When Usain won his first gold medal over 100 metres in Beijing it reminded me of the film *The Matrix* where Morpheous says of Neo, 'He's beginning to believe.'

CHAPTER 6

GETTING SERIOUS

THE RELATIONSHIP BETWEEN TYSON GAY AND me has changed since I started setting world records. At the World Championships in Osaka, Japan in 2007 my focus was on trying to match Tyson, who was in tremendous form and the man to beat over both the 100 and 200 metres. At that time I accepted he was better than me and we got along great. It's not the same now that I'm beating him. Maybe that's natural, but my improved performances never affected my relationship with Wallace Spearmon, who is one of the coolest guys on the circuit, and we still chill out and enjoy playing video games together.

To get in shape for challenging Tyson, I wanted to be running as many races as possible. My injury troubles were over after a frustrating two and a half years and I needed to earn some money to make a living. Although the 200 metres was not a major event on the circuit, I was ranked high enough to be able to command those big appearance fees. At a Golden League meeting, which unfortunately didn't include the 200 metres very often because the 100 metres was deemed more glamorous, you might get another 15,000 dollars for winning, 10,000 for second and so on. If you won all six Golden League races – as my Jamaican team-mate Asafa Powell did in the 100 metres in 2006 – you shared in a 750,000 dollar jackpot.

Going into Osaka I was rather under the radar. No one was looking for too much from me, which I was quite happy about. All the Jamaican attention was fixed on Asafa, who had some injury troubles but was the world 100m record holder and had just won two Golden League meetings.

We were out there around midday for the heats of the 200 metres, and I eased through in second place while a Greek runner beside me almost burst a blood vessel to beat me by one hundredth of a second. The quarter-finals were the same day in the evening and I won my race, with Wallace just behind, but it was interesting to see that Tyson ran quite a quick time, almost going under 20 seconds. The semi-final the next night had me and Wallace again in the same race. We qualified first and second but Tyson was the fastest, bang on the 20-second mark.

I went to bed thinking about the final the following day and how I was going to tackle it. Tyson was a fast bend runner, whereas I wasn't as quick. I tended to lean into the corner, when the best way to do it is to stay up straight.

I did as well as I possibly could in the final. Coach said it was one of the fastest corners I'd had ever run, but Tyson was leading me by about three metres, winning in a time of 19.76 to my 19.91. There was nothing I could do other than to hang to the silver medal position and hold off Wallace. Getting silver was good. I'd shown, at last, that I could produce in a major championships. While it seemed I'd been around a long time, I was only 21 with a lot to learn. Tyson was 25 with more experience than me. In an interview afterwards I held my hands up and agreed Tyson was the best man on the day. He was in the shape of his life and had done the sprint double, having also beaten Asafa into third place in the 100 metres.

At Osaka I got another silver in the 4x100 metres relay in which, although Asafa ran his heart out on the last leg, we lost to the USA while edging out Great Britain by one hundredth of a second. We had plenty of speed in our team and broke the Jamaican national record, but our baton changing was absolutely useless, we must have messed up

every handover. As a country we only have ourselves to blame for that, because we never practise relays before a competition and don't have proper training camps like the British and the US do. Our preparation consists of doing a couple of baton passes when we get there and hoping it works out on the night. If you look at Jamaican baton changes over the years they've been alright at best, never good or great. We get our results through sheer speed and are forever making up lost ground.

Back home the reaction to my silvers showed that people were warming to me, but it wasn't like they were saying, 'Hey, brilliant' – it was more 'You're getting there' – and there were more comments about my love of the party lifestyle. Basically the argument went that if I didn't go clubbing I would be winning gold medals.

That wasn't the reason. I just wasn't strong enough yet, because I hadn't been doing the full training. While Mr Coleman had got me doing too much gym work, now I wasn't doing any and it meant I didn't have the stamina to complete the 200 metres properly – 20 to 30 metres out I was dying. Coach said I was too weak, and it was what we must work on for the 2008 Olympics.

I'd been going on at Mr Mills for a while about doing the 100 metres as well as the 200 like Tyson, partly because there was big money to be earned and the 200 metres was the poor relation by comparison. But Coach had this thing about me doing the 400 metres, which I wasn't keen on. There was a stand-off, which left me sticking to one event because neither of us could convince the other about what my second discipline should be.

We made a bet that if I did well in a 100m race in Crete, Greece, before the World Championships he would let me double up in 100 and 200 metres the following season. If I didn't do well I would do 400 and 200. Training for the 400 metres struck me as hell on earth, so I wasn't going to blow this opportunity. My time of 10.03 in that first ever senior 100 metres was impressive. The only person in Jamaica running faster than that was Asafa, so I told Coach he had to give me the chance.

Mr Mills said he always knew I could run the 100 metres but never wanted me to. He thought I was a more natural quarter-miler, but I didn't want to do 400 because of the different type of training, which is severely hard. I see what these guys have to do when we are training with my team, Racers Track Club in Kingston. In one session the quarter-milers can be running two 600s, two 500s, one 350 and four 300s. That's a lot of work. You are doing 1200 metres, then 1000 metres, then a 350, then 1200 again, which is crazy. I don't think I'm made for so much work in one day.

I can run 45 seconds for 400 metres without doing any of that, which shows I have a lot of talent. But I would have to put the work in if I was going to break the world record, it couldn't be done without any specific training. I'm capable of the 400m world record but I'm

not ready for that yet, I want to keep on with the 100 and 200 metres and leave it at that. The 400 metres might be for the 2016 Olympics after I've defended my titles in London, but I will never, ever go any further than that. You will not see Usain Bolt doing an 800 metres, it would kill me.

It wasn't until that silver in Japan that it struck me I could be a great athlete. I hadn't been doing the core gym work which was the staple training of so many athletes, and I'd still finished second. I knew that if I put my heart into it, I could be the best in the world at 100 and 200.

In only my third 100 metres as a professional athlete, in May 2008, I ran 9.76 seconds during a meet at Kingston's national stadium – just two hundredths of a second slower than Asafa's world record. I'd predicted a run of about 9.9 and the time blew me away. I was shocked, and the legendary Michael Johnson said he was amazed at my improvement. There were accusations in the States that the run wasn't legal, and that with it being in Jamaica there had to be some questions about it, like the clock not working correctly.

Whatever they thought, our minds were made up that I would run both the 100 and 200 metres at the Beijing Olympics. We didn't make it public, though, saying no decision had been made and that I might only do the 200 because Coach was worried whether my body could cope with both disciplines.

When I went to the Reebok Grand Prix in New York at the end of May I wasn't thinking about breaking a world record. This was business, taking on Tyson Gay over 100 metres for the first time. If the athletics world had doubts about me, this was the place to put them right.

I was determined not to let Tyson beat me. I'd put in the hours at the gym, working on my abs and doing all the exercises to get stronger. The only worry was my start, but Tyson was not the best starter either so we were even on that one.

There had been heavy rain beforehand, but that can be good. As long as a track is not soaking wet it is bouncier when it's damp. I noticed I was missing a spike in my left shoe, which wasn't unusual for me; I also had one missing in the Olympic final a few months later. I don't know why it happens, they just go, and then the hole gets clogged up and you cannot fit a new spike in to replace the old one. It's not a disaster to lose one, because there are seven more and they are all at the top of the running shoe, whereas if you lose a stud in a football boot it has more effect. Ideally, though, you should run with all spikes in and having one less is not going to help you.

When the gun went I made a better start than Tyson, got ahead of him, and knew from that position on he wasn't going to pass me. I kept

going, going, going and wasn't even looking at the clock when I crossed the line. I wasn't thinking records, just that I'd beaten Tyson Gay. This was a very bright flash of the Lightning Bolt.

I didn't find out I'd set the world record – of 9.72 seconds , beating Asafa's mark by two-hundreths – until I was jogging along the back straight and it was announced over the public address system. I beat my chest and was like 'yes'. Anything was possible now and the bonus was it had shut those people up who said it wasn't a proper clock in Jamaica. The Americans could see it for themselves now, it was right in front of them. Tyson offered his congratulations, we shook hands and did an interview together. But our relationship was never the same again, and that's down to him not me.

You have to do the Olympic trials no matter how good you are, even if you are a world record holder. You cannot skip them unless you have a good reason, like an injury, but they are easy enough, there are rarely any surprises and the same people usually make the team. I always try to win and keep my unbeaten record up, and I was happy to beat Asafa in the 100 metres.

We moved over to England, where my agent, Ricky Simms, who books all my meetings, is based. He would organise accommodation in Teddington, on the Thames near London, and the Racers Track Club members stay there for the big European races along with Ricky's other clients from around the world. There are many different nationalities, and you get to meet people who ordinarily you might not have much to do with.

Asafa beat me at an IAAF grand prix event in Stockholm before the Olympics. It was a result which created a media stir, but it was down to my bad start and didn't give me any doubts about winning golds in Beijing. There are different starters at the meetings who all have their own ways. There are fast starters and slow starters, and you get to know them after a while and how they do it. In Stockholm the guy waits until everybody gets up on the word 'set' before he fires. I was up and waiting and waiting for a good three seconds wondering what the heck was going on, and when he fired I had lost concentration and was caught off guard day-dreaming. I ran hard to get back at Asafa, who was looking over his shoulder, but for some reason I didn't want to win, didn't want it enough. If I'd leaned forward I would have won. I was catching Asafa and he was tightening. Coach asked me first if I was giving out Christmas presents early and then said he was happy about what happened, because it would teach me to get serious and get focused. Like he said, you have to learn how to lose and why you lost.

I didn't race Asafa after that until the Olympics; nor did I compete against Tyson either. Asafa had beaten me once, I'd beaten Tyson, and Tyson had beaten Asafa. Asafa and I were going to race a few days later at Crystal Palace in London, but Coach decided against it, saying, 'Let's keep them confident.'

We were playing games, keeping our opponents guessing, but we knew I was ready for Beijing.

" WE WERE PLAYING GAMES, KEEPING OUR OPPONENTS GUESSING, BUT WE KNEW I WAS READY FOR BEIJING "

GLEN MILLS

COACH

I remember seeing this tall, lanky athlete at age 14 competing at the annual track and field championships in Kingston and it brought back some memories of the late Arthur Wint and Herb McKenley. I thought, 'Is he to be one of the best Jamaica has ever seen?'

As a coach with over 40 years' experience, there is always some hope to have a talent of Usain's ability to work with. I got that chance and it has been an interesting journey. I feel the world will experience a lot more of what I think Usain can do, but we are focused on the commitment, discipline and dedication it will take to make that happen. While being conscious that he has not maximised his true potential, I think he is a fantastic athlete – once in a lifetime you see this kind of talent.

Jamaica has had a rich tradition of producing world beaters. Usain has carried on that tradition in a time much different from when McKenley and Wint competed in the late 1940s and 50s; an era that characterised the domination of sprinting of black athletes from developing countries.

More opportunities always used to be available for our athletes if they went to seek better training facilities in the USA and UK, but we have found a formula which has helped to prepare Usain and other elite athletes in Jamaica. Asafa Powell and then

Usain stayed in Jamaica and showed there was a better way for our athletes to develop. Previously none had been prepared to take that chance, now you can see the quality coming through.

My attitude towards coaching is not one-dimensional, it is also geared towards acquiring life skills. From that standpoint, whoever I've trained, I've tried to get them to understand the skills and values in life, so that they not only fulfil their potential as athletes but are also balanced people. My philosophy is that you can reach them so much better if you come across not just as their teacher but as their friend. Usain is just unique. From day one, he has always been a joy to handle, even in challenging times. He doesn't always follow all instructions, but his personality is one which will not allow you to be angry with him for too long. My relationship with Usain is extremely close, like father to son. Wherever he is in the world, if I'm not there, he will call me to ask if I'm OK. If he sees me looking like I'm under pressure, he wants to know what it's all about and how he can help to make it better.

Words are inadequate to describe the rough times we had at the beginning, but the results today are an indication that you may find water in the middle of a desert.

Usain came to me after a disappointing

performance at the 2004 Summer Olympics. He then pulled up in the 200 metres in the 2005 World Championships in Helsinki. Those two performances were to signal his arrival in the big leagues having had the pressure of being a junior star.

It was painful for him and he'd get bad comments from people in the street. There were cartoons in the paper and he faced strong criticism in the media. My job was to refocus his attention to recover. I tried to convince him that if he was patient it would all work out.

I too got criticism from the media, with them questioning my ability and calling for a new coach. I told him to be confident in himself and not to let external forces affect him. Even when I, his coach, believed that he could rise above the adversities, the onus would be on him to believe.

We had a short to medium-term plan lasting a few years, and I knew that when we were successful it would all change. One of the plans was not to hide him from his major competitors, who at the time were Tyson Gay and Wallace Spearmon. I faced some fierce opposition to that decision, with no one seeming to understand the method to my madness. But I felt he needed to compete against the top contenders at that time, if he was to become the best.

They thought I should hide him, but he needed to run against the people he was going to challenge. We were in the learning process, and I told Usain the technical skills that we were developing would result in ultimate success.

While the rest of the world condemned us, following his numerous defeats, I felt assured that my strategy was justified, as Usain did not question my method. Usain was committed to the plan and we pursued it vigorously.

When the transformation began, the rest of the world was shocked. One European coach, who had studied and analysed Usain, was amazed at the turnaround. He was very specific in his comments regarding how Usain used to lean back when he was running, but that everything had been revolutionised. He asked how I'd done it and I told him, 'It took faith, hard work and the technical knowledge I acquired over the years in sprinting.'

Usain placed a lot of faith in me and what I told him. Thank God I went down the right path and that now he's executing most of what I've taught him. He has been able to perform and show his true talent and will continue to do amazing things. We are about 75 per cent along the way of what we're aiming to do, but a major part of what we still have to do is to develop a greater degree of explosive strength. His strength factor still isn't where it ought to be.

Usain's preparation is a lot more technical than the typical sprinter because of his height. You have to know the right amount of work to give him and when to back off, because otherwise he could get hurt. He's the best talent I've ever worked with, but it's not a walk in the park. His current training and competition programme is aimed towards him staying healthy over the rest of his career. As a result we have to plan his competition schedule meticulously for each season.

I laugh when people say Mills can't coach and that Usain is just a tremendous talent. He is, but if they knew how difficult and challenging it is to get him ready to run those races they would have a greater understanding of the task at hand.

I can work out from our programme how fast he might run, and it's not a surprise when he does it. We knew from our final preparation before the Berlin World Championships that his time could improve if he executed the plan correctly. We improved his starting performance in the 100 metres, by making certain changes in his body position on the blocks. In 2009 he was leading after 20 metres, whereas previously he didn't get into the lead until after 60 metres, and that's testimony to the technical work being done.

One of my philosophies is that you never stop learning. So I always listen to what others have to say, professional or otherwise. I've acquired a lot of knowledge over the years, and now I'm trying to pass it on to my young coaching staff, so that we can continue to produce more athletes like Usain.

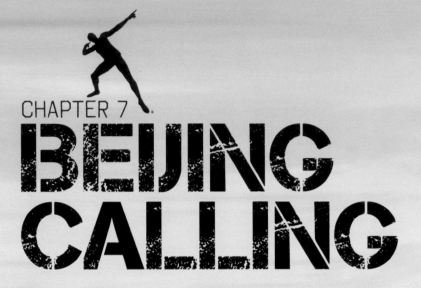

CHAPTER 7
BEIJING CALLING

AS WE FLEW TO CHINA AND THE excitement of the Olympics was building, I felt so good that I recorded myself on my cell phone saying, 'I'm going to win three gold medals.' It wasn't being boastful, I really believed it.

There's a picture on the wall in my Aunty Lilly's front room that confirms the great shape I was in. It was taken by a press photographer and shows me and Glen Mills at the training camp outside Beijing when he was going through starts with me. My muscles are rippling and I love that look.

We were in China for two weeks before the Games, but the training camp was about four hours outside Beijing. Twice we had to drive into the city by bus, once for a Puma party and another time to sort out accreditation. It was not an enjoyable experience, but once we got into the village, everything was perfect.

I had the ideal man to train with in my Racers Club team-mate Daniel Bailey, who represents Antigua. Daniel won a bronze at the 2010 World Indoor Championships over 60 metres and is renowned as one of the best starters in the business. If you can get out of the blocks before him, you know your starts are alright. One day I got him four times and he was really annoyed about it. That told me everything was coming together nicely.

There had been a lot of warnings about smog, which notoriously hangs over the industrial city of Beijing for weeks on end. Coach was worried about it, but when we arrived we hardly saw any. They must have closed down every factory for miles.

So the atmosphere in the air was good, as was the atmosphere in the athletes' village. One of the joys of athletics is to spend time messing around with your friends, and there is plenty of time to do that at an Olympics. I'm not one who would rather stay in a hotel away from it all;

I like to get into the whole scene, because there's always something going on. We play video games, cards and dominoes, talk for hours and go for walks round the village to check out the hot girls from other countries. I've even started learning Spanish, because if I have another language I'll be able to speak to a lot more ladies instead of just staring at them. You can get by on Spanish with the Portuguese speakers as the languages are quite similar, which is good news when it comes to the Brazilian beauties. I wish I'd learned Spanish at school, but I didn't get along with the teacher so I switched and did music instead. I'm not going to start singing to the girls, though.

Unfortunately sprinters, of all the athletes, are the ones who can least afford to be distracted by the pleasures of the opposite sex while at the Olympics. As a sprinter you start the heats on the first day of the athletics programme and, if you run in the 4x100 metres relay as I do, you don't finish until near the end of the Games. You are lucky if you get two decent nights' partying in, although we go for it once we are off the leash.

Nobody is more important than anyone else in the athletes' village. Everyone is equal. You cannot help looking around to spot famous faces. I remember seeing the Chinese basketball star, Yao Ming, at the 2004 Olympics and feeling like a dwarf. I'm 6ft 5ins but he is 7ft 6ins, and I had to arch my neck to look at him. In Beijing I was looking downwards at the man next door, the little Argentinian football genius, Lionel Messi.

Before the 100m heats there had been stories that Tyson was struggling with injury. That was obviously going to increase my chances of success, but I had to concentrate on what I was doing and not take any notice. If I performed at my best, no one was going to beat me anyway.

Waking early on day one of the athletics competition I felt no nerves, just excitement. I headed to breakfast at McDonald's for my regular bowl of chicken nuggets. Honestly, I ate nothing else in all my time out in China except chicken nuggets. They were the only food I could properly trust which wouldn't affect my stomach. On arriving at the training camp I'd tried a local Chinese meal, which wasn't like the ones we eat in the West, and my body didn't react well. So, knowing I could rely on nuggets, I made up my mind that was all I would eat. And eat them I did, 15 at a time, for breakfast, lunch and dinner, washed down with bottled water.

It was 10 o'clock in the morning and the sun was already burning down as I lined up for my first 100m heat in the magnificent Bird's Nest Stadium. There would be no trouble qualifying and no need to worry about false starts. I was comfortably faster than my opponents, which meant I didn't have to get out of the blocks too quick. Once the gun went I cruised it in 10.2, while Tyson won his heat too, which made me wonder about those injury stories.

The first two rounds of the 100 metres were on the same day, but with about a ten-hour gap in between. So, with a lot of time to kill, I returned to the village for more nuggets and a few hours' sleep. I won my quarter-final in 9.92, easing down and doing my usual trick of looking around all over the place, but was still the fastest qualifier. Tyson qualified ninth, and now I was thinking it might be true about the injury.

When I'm running well it doesn't feel like any effort, it's smooth, almost peaceful, and when I rang NJ that night I told him I was feeling confident. My room-mate Maurice Smith, the decathlete, was also

" WHEN I AM RUNNING WELL IT DOESN'T FEEL LIKE ANY EFFORT, IT'S SMOOTH, ALMOST PEACEFUL. "

keeping me relaxed. I'd asked him to room with me because we went back a good few years together and I enjoyed his company. We had a lot of fun and would never go to sleep, like kids on a camp. His event didn't start for a few days, so he was happy to stay up and chat and was forever filming things. He's got hours of footage from our time in Beijing, and whenever I see him we love to sit and watch it all again. Coach was next door and got annoyed that we'd never go to bed. One night he came to our room and told us off like schoolboys because we were up until 2am laughing. I was so disappointed for Maurice when it went wrong for him in the rain on the first day of the decathlon. He did better on day two, but he was too far behind. He'd trained so well in the lead-up to the Games, and I was willing him to succeed because he was such a help to me.

The semi-finals and final of the 100 metres were the day after the heats, and Tyson's injury problem was confirmed when he finished fifth in his semi – well behind Asafa – and failed to make the final. I focused on getting my start right and won my semi in 9.85, which was six hundredths faster than Asafa in spite of easing down in the last 20 metres.

The people of Beijing seemed to be loving me. They generated so much positive energy in my direction and their enthusiasm was infectious. I felt very comfortable, and in the two and a half hours before the final I was aware of a lot of talk about whether I could break my own world record. You could feel it in the air.

There was no time to go back to the village, so I just hung around talking to Coach and having a laugh. Some athletes go through every aspect of the race and analyse it in detail, not me. Coach might mention one or two things, but we don't dwell on it.

It was hot but I was well hydrated, having started a programme a month before which made sure my fluid intake was correct at all times. There's no danger of cramp as long as you stay hydrated and, while I have a full-time masseur who travels with me, I don't like to have too many massages unless my legs are really tight.

There were TVs in the warm-up area, where I watched the other events as well as re-runs of Asafa's and my semis. I was happy with what I saw and felt sure that, as long as my start was OK, I would win my first Olympic gold medal. The 100 metres felt like child's play, it was a bit of a hobby. The 200 metres was the real deal, being the more technical event where you have to work on the corner and, as it was twice as long, there was the possibility you could tire in the closing stages. In the 100 metres I was hardly blowing, it was so easy, but then again I'd put the training in, which is maybe why I felt so good. When it comes to competition there is a different feeling from training. The adrenalin kicks in and, if you've done it right, you will fly.

I was disappointed Tyson didn't make the final, because I wanted every rival out there. This wasn't like the world juniors, when I was pleased the best runners were missing. Now I thrived on the competition and didn't want anyone saying I only won because Tyson had an injury. I don't like unfinished business with a rival, I'd rather get it done. There had been so much said about our re-match in Beijing and now it wasn't going to happen. It shouldn't have mattered, because if you win it goes in the record books and there's no asterisk beside it or note saying, 'Didn't count. Main rival wasn't in race.' A gold is a gold, but I'd still rather Tyson had made it.

The minutes ticked by, the final got closer, and Asafa, who had a reputation for nerves, was getting edgy. There was a lot of pressure on him. Although he was one of the world's great sprinters and held the 100m record for three years before me, he had never won a major title and some commentators were hinting that he lacked mental strength.

I genuinely felt for him and wanted to help loosen him up. This was a fellow Jamaican and a friend I admired, and he chilled a little as we had a laugh with the other three Caribbean competitors in the final, another Jamaican, Michael Frater, and two guys from Trinidad, Marc Burns and Richard Thompson.

Then it was time for business. We made the walk out to the track and I was happy and relaxed, taking it all in, thinking about different kinds of stuff like video games, and what I was going to do after the championships. I felt calm – there was no fear. If I got a reasonable start I was going to be OK, I would win. I took a look at the finish line and settled down into the blocks.

Bang! The moment the gun went I checked out my rivals as I popped the blocks, glancing left and right to see whether they'd got out before me. It was just a quick scan of the area as I made the first step in lane four, but Thompson and Walter Dix had got away quickest,

I WAS STILL LOOKING TO MY RIGHT AS I THUMPED MY CHEST AND CROSSED THE LINE

blocking my view of Asafa who was in lane seven. My reaction time was seventh quickest of the eight finalists, but as I completed my first stride I was right up there with everyone else, and by the second step I was ahead and thinking, 'Got it.' I stumbled slightly on my fifth step, which stopped me looking across again, but once I got into my drive phase, I was moving well. By 55 metres I was going away from the pack, and by 85 metres I knew for certain I'd won it. Nobody was going to pass me now. The only person who was even close to running the times I'd been doing was Asafa, and I couldn't see him on my right.

I wasn't thinking world records, just feeling the sheer happiness of winning that gold medal. I eased up, stretched out my arms and was still looking to my right as I thumped my chest and crossed the line. I didn't see the clock – or notice that my lace had come loose and I could have tripped over.

The spectators were on their feet, flash bulbs exploded round the stadium and, on my lap of honour, I pointed both arms skywards mimicking the actions of a bolt being fired. It wasn't a pre-planned action like when I practised my breakdancing before the world youths, it was totally spontaneous. It was now the signature of the world's fastest man.

CHRISTINE BOLT-HYLTON

HALF-SISTER

I'm four years older than Usain and we were in and out of each other's lives when we were kids. I lived with my mom for a while, then moved in with Dad and Jennifer, and then went back to my mom's, but I would still visit Dad's every month.

Usain is like all brothers, he can be a pain sometimes. We would argue over games we were playing or what we were watching on TV. He would tease me, saying my belly was too big.

We would race each other up the hill to the shop, but he was faster than me by the time he was in grade five. I'd have to tug his shirt or push him down to win. I was quite into sports, and we had bets on the cricket about who was going to win, and I'd join in with his cricket and football games.

Because of Usain's lack of experience in the 100 metres I bet against my Dad, saying Usain would not win the Olympic 100 metres. I even placed a bet of US$100 against my Dad; so I got the surprise of my life.

I was so sure of the 200 metres win, and all of us in the house agreed he would be the clear winner. I even went as far as to say he would break the 200 metres world record, and that he did. While my dad thought he would win, he did not expect world records ... I am still waiting to collect from him.

It was overwhelming to watch, trust me. It was amazing to know it was my little brother out there doing such things. The moment he won the 100 metres, cars came out all over Trelawny and drove round honking their horns. When he won the 200 metres there were even more cars and more noise.

Since Usain won the World Championships and broke the world records again I can honestly say there is nothing I don't expect from him on the track. Everything is possible. If he ran eight seconds for the 100 metres I wouldn't be surprised.

It can be good and bad having a famous brother. It has changed my life in that I'm more in the spotlight, which can sometimes be quite nice but not always. You can be out with friends and when people realise you're Usain's sister they'll say, 'Give me money.' When I say I don't have much money, they'll go, 'But you're the sister of the fastest man in the world, you must have money.'

Usain is a good brother. My five-year-old daughter Sherunda worships him and he spoils her. Everywhere she goes she tells people, 'Usain Bolt is my uncle.' She's a female version of Usain. She's going to be an athlete just like him.

CHAPTER 8

ON TOP OF THE WORLD

I HAD NO IDEA I'D BROKEN THE world record. How could I have broken it? I was slowing down long before the finish and wasn't tired at all. I could have gone back to the start and done it all over again.

I ran round the track looking for Mom and Mr Peart. They had told me they would be on the back straight, but I didn't know where exactly, and it was only when they called out 'VJ!' that I was able to find them. Dad hadn't come, because he didn't like long-haul flights, but Mom had fought her way down to the front. I gave her a big hug while Mr Peart was slapping me on the back, and then some other guy squeezed me as hard as he could. I didn't know who he was and had to wrestle quite hard to get away from him. He must have had a big bet on me.

I didn't know where Coach Mills was in the stadium, but I knew he would be a happy man. I stopped to celebrate with Marion and Ricky from PACE Sports Management – who were on the home straight. I could tell by then that everyone was proud of my achievement.

Only when I'd got right round the Bird's Nest and back to the finish line did I realise the time was 9.69 seconds, beating my previous world record by three hundredths. All the photographers were knocking each other over wanting a picture of me and the clock and shouting, 'It's a record, it's a record.' For me the Olympics had been about winning, nothing else, but to do it in record time was special.

Michael Johnson, who was commentating for the BBC in Britain, was saying that Michael Phelps, the swimmer who won eight gold medals in Beijing the previous week, was now 'Michael who?' because what I'd done was greater. I didn't see it like that. I wasn't competing with Phelps for superstardom. What he did was phenomenal and deserved to stand separately in its own right.

I did all the media afterwards which took me forever. I stopped for everybody, knowing how important this was for the broadcasters. There was no avoiding a camera or a microphone. There were TV guys on three levels, with six cameras on each level, and I had to

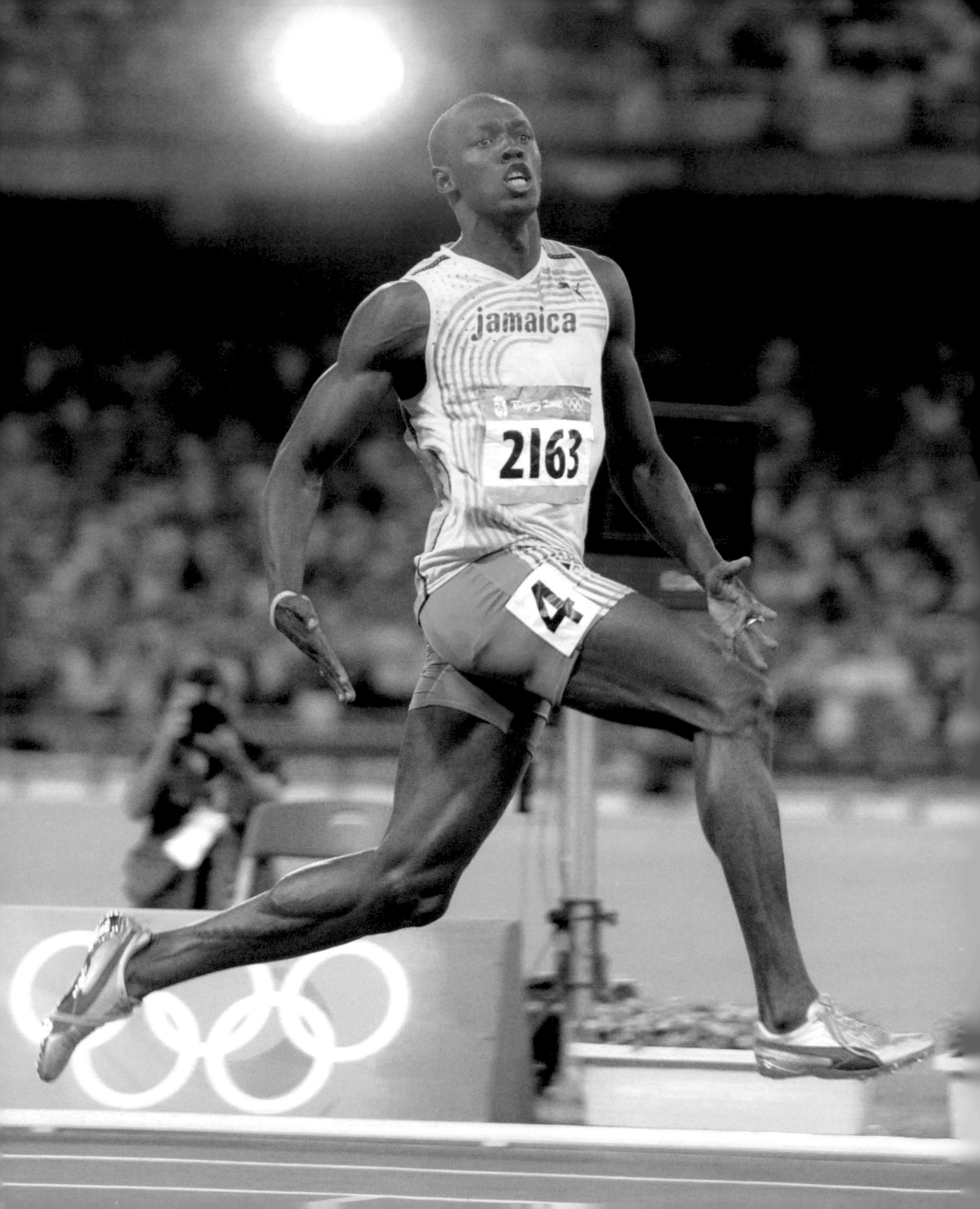
jamaica
2163
4

spend a few minutes with each. Then there were the radio people on the top level, and others further outside. I did nearly an hour of that, then had to go and see the newspaper guys, so it probably took me about an hour and a half in all.

Everyone asked what time I could have run if I hadn't slowed down. I couldn't answer. I didn't know. What did it matter anyway? I'd won the gold medal.

The evening was still not over. There was compulsory drug testing, and producing a sample took some doing, I can tell you. I must have been there over an hour. The rules require that a chaperone stays with you from the race finish to the moment you produce the sample. It's a strange job but someone has to do it, and I'd got used to that sort of unusual attention, having become the most tested athlete in history, in my view.

Some of the testers really watch you closely, and when you first go through it, it is really uncomfortable having a guy staring while you are trying to pee. To prove you aren't up to any tricks you have to lift your shirt right up, and some want you to pull your pants down too. It's a bit weird, not great fun.

Ricky and I were alone for the drug testing, Coach had gone, and all the lights were off. They had to get us a car because the shuttle buses had stopped too. It was a surreal end to it all from the euphoria in the stadium to total quiet.

By the time my post-race duties were done it was well after midnight and the stadium was closed up as I headed back to the village. Before that I stopped by Ricky's apartment where Mom, Mizicann and Mr Peart were staying. Ricky had a big grin on his face the whole evening: his phone was ringing off the hook with people calling to congratulate me and the media looking to set up interviews. On the way home we called Dad and NJ in Jamaica, who filled me in on the celebrations that were going on back home.

As soon as I got back to the village the first thing I did was to get some chicken nuggets down me. What else? I was starving. It must have been one in the morning and there was hardly anyone in the restaurant either, so I took my nuggets back to my room. Coach Mills and my masseur Eddie were there. After all, the hard work had paid off. I was then joking with Coach about some things I could do to improve on my race. Celebrations were happening all around. I was happy, though, to have the people around me who work so hard to support me in what I do.

The Jamaicans who weren't competing were waiting to congratulate me. Then I saw Maurice, who had stayed up to say 'well done' and immediately got his camera out to do an interview with me. I went to sleep a very contented man.

The medal presentation was not until late evening the next day and there was nothing else to do except put my feet up. I saw the race replayed on TV, but couldn't get it on the internet because YouTube seemed to be blocked. My team-mates were asking how come I could slow down so much and still win, which is what the TV interviewers had been saying too.

It was pretty amazing to have done that and still set a world record, and when I watched it again even I was surprised how far out I'd eased up. I heard people accusing me of disrespect to my rivals, and I thought, 'Oh shit, maybe I shouldn't have done that.' It wasn't on purpose, and never for a moment did I mean it as an insult to my fellow athletes, but the excitement of knowing I was going to win had taken me over.

" I WAS SLOWING DOWN LONG BEFORE THE FINISH AND WASN'T TIRED AT ALL. I COULD HAVE GONE BACK TO THE START AND DONE IT ALL OVER AGAIN "

The head of the International Olympic Committee, Jacques Rogge, told the press, 'That's not the way we perceive being a champion,' and that I should have shown more respect. My behaviour was becoming a bigger story than the victory, so I asked a few of the guys from the race what they thought. They said 'No, man, it's fine, you won, you were happy, do whatever you want,' which made me feel better. If it was OK by them, what did it matter what anyone else thought?

The medal presentation was brilliant. The stadium was packed and the cheers from the spectators were deafening. As the Jamaican flag was raised and the national anthem, 'Land We Love', played, I was singing and smiling about the fact that the guys were willing me to turn the tears on when I got on that podium.

There was no danger. I'm not emotional that way. Of course, I wasn't finished with the Olympics, far from it. It was straight back to work with the heats of the 200 metres the following morning. I felt fresh, not drained at all by the 100m experience. I'd been running the fastest 200m times by far in the lead-up to the Games; there was no Tyson because of his injury; and I was confident that my motto 'Once I beat you, you will not beat me again' would ensure I held off any challenge by Wallace Spearmon.

I was second in my heat behind a Trinidad guy called Rondell Sorrillo who was busting his chops to beat me. There was no point taking him on, it meant more to him than me and, as it turned out, he didn't even make it through to the semis.

I won my quarter-final with little difficulty, then qualified fastest for the final, running 20.09 in what was a strong semi ahead of the US pair of Shawn Crawford and Wallace.

In truth I was more confident of winning the 200 metres than I had been in the 100, though by now I was beginning to feel the effects of the week. When the media asked about the prospects of me breaking another world record, I said, 'No, I'm just going to take it easy.' My energy was sapped.

To my amazement, the next morning I felt totally refreshed and told Maurice I would run my heart out, give it everything and see what happened. There would be no slowing down in the last 20 metres, it would be full out to the line, not because of the criticism I'd had but because I felt good enough to have a shot at the record.

This was no ordinary record. Michael Johnson had set his 200m mark of 19.32 seconds at the 1996 Games in Atlanta. It had stood for so long that many had thought it unbeatable, including me. Johnson was the man in the 200, the number one athlete I looked up to in an event

which had always been my main goal. The 100 metres was for fun, the 200 metres was my job.

I had lane five, so there would be no tight bend, and I was so relaxed I did a few of my new Bolt signature moves while my name was being announced. All I had to do was get away smoothly, which I did, and coming off the corner I was well clear. Now it was all about pushing to get that record. I hadn't been bothered about getting the 100m record, just the gold medal, but I wanted this record. As I powered over the line I looked straight at the clock and knew it was mine —19.30.

Johnson had said on TV that he thought I wouldn't be able to break the record. He didn't think I had the endurance to sustain my speed to the line, but afterwards he called me Superman II and praised my start, which was especially pleasing.

I didn't know what to do to celebrate. I was going to whip my shirt off, but you're not allowed to do that. So, after lying flat on the track to get my breath for a second, I got up and did a few dances, then answered the call to 'do that Lightning Bolt thing'. Oh yes, Lightning had struck twice.

Winning the 200 metres and breaking the record was better than the 100, because all the time I was growing up I never thought it possible. A lot of guys coming out of the States were capable of running 19.7 and 19.6, which I had done too, and it seemed to be the barrier no one could get below. But that day, at that moment, it clicked with me. The track was fast, I was in the best shape of my life, and my mind told me to go out there and leave everything on the track. Unlike in the 100, I'd had to dig deep, very deep, and was absolutely dead afterwards.

I recovered for the presentation the following day – and it didn't get much better than that. I was on top of the podium with the Jamaican flag fluttering, it was my 22nd birthday and 91,000 people were singing 'Happy Birthday' in English. What an experience that was!

The heats of the 4x100 metres were the same day, and I watched as Jamaica qualified, having been given the luxury of sitting it out

until the final. Then the big question was whether the relay would produce my third world record. I doubted it, not because I didn't believe in my team-mates – it was me I wasn't sure about.

I was on the third leg to run the corner, but the baton changing was far from perfect and Michael Frater almost ran out of his lane as he handed it on to me. When I do the 4x100, I usually pull away from the others, but not this time. I was tired and just about kept us going, then Asafa slipped as he was moving off, which meant I had to slow down to get the baton to him safely.

But, once Asafa was away, it was a beautiful sight. My favourite picture ever is of Asafa flying and me screaming at him to go hard for the line. I knew nobody was going to beat us, that the record was in sight, and I chased him all the way down the track as we clocked 37.10 and broke the world mark by three tenths of a second. It was party time.

I had to do all the usual interviews and drug tests, but we got out by midnight and headed for a club called China Doll for our big night out. There was only champagne available, no beer, so the fizzy stuff it was. We got the Jamaican beat going, started dancing, and drank Moët almost till the sun came up.

It was about 5.30am when the cab dropped us back at the village. I could have slept forever, yet no sooner had my head hit the pillow than I had to get up again. There was a press conference scheduled for that morning, and my agent Ricky was pouring Red Bull down my neck to get me back into the land of the living. I wore dark glasses to stop the sun hurting my eyes as we made our way to the interview, but once in there the glasses came off and I perked up. Thanks, Ricky.

There was another party that evening hosted by our sponsors, Puma, and it was good to see Dad there enjoying himself. He'd put his fear of flying behind him to come out after Digicel persuaded him and paid for his trip. He still didn't get to the stadium in time to see the 200m final, but at least he saw the 4x100 metres.

As the night wore on me and my girlfriend Mizicann slipped off to a hotel for a more private celebration. I felt like I'd earned it.

" I WANTED THIS RECORD. AS
I POWERED OVER THE LINE
I LOOKED STRAIGHT AT THE
CLOCK AND KNEW IT
WAS MINE..."

CHAPTER 9
HOMECOMING

HAVING FILMED MYSELF FLYING INTO BEIJING predicting I'd win three gold medals, it was only right I filmed myself flying out with them hanging round my neck. It was to be my personal proof that what I say is what I do.

What gets me annoyed is that I'll never see those pictures again, thanks to the idiots who stole my trusty Nokia N95 phone at a party in Kingston. I was driving out of the car park and these guys stopped to ask for my autograph, blocking me in. I thought it weird the way they leaned in through the side window, and as soon as they went something didn't feel right. When I looked down I realised they'd taken the phone from the compartment in the side door. If anyone reading this knows where that phone is, I'd love to have it back, no questions asked.

I followed my Olympic success by winning over 100 metres in Zurich, which was not bad after a few days' partying. I then won the 200 metres in Lausanne and a 100m race in Brussels. After that I'd had enough. It was time to go home and see my people.

Everyone in Jamaica seemed to know the day – 8 September – and time – 1.15pm – that I was due to land at Norman Manley airport in Kingston. What a welcome! There were thousands there to greet me, many of whom had spilled on to the tarmac. The Prime Minister of Jamaica, Bruce Golding, the opposition leader Portia Simpson Miller and the sports minister Olivia Grange met me at the steps, while a BMW convertible waited to take me on to a reception in the centre of Kingston. The convertible might have seemed like a good idea, but it meant everyone could grab me and pull my arms. Luckily the rain came down, so we had to pull the top up, which saved me from being torn to pieces.

When you drive from the airport there is a big roundabout, and that day you couldn't even see it because there were so many people standing there, even though they were getting soaking wet. The car

came to a complete stop and hordes of fans were banging on the roof and the windows. One little girl forced her hand in through the window and shouted to me, 'I'm going to be the next Usain Bolt.' We were stuck for half an hour until the police managed to clear the way and we travelled on through Mountain View. In town the streets were lined with happy Jamaicans who could not have cared less about the weather.

Eventually we made it to the Pegasus Hotel, but it was impossible to get through the front door and the police had to clear the reception

area too. It was truly mad. I never expected a homecoming like it. Nobody was bothered about my party lifestyle now – this was one party where everyone wanted to be.

When I won the world juniors I got a lot of attention, but this was something else. My arms were scratched where everyone had clawed at me, and there was a danger of events getting out of control. I was supposed to be staying at the Pegasus, but had to move to another hotel because I couldn't go out of the door without being mobbed. When I went clubbing that night, security had to rescue me from being crushed. I'd gone in through the back entrance and they'd prepared a special table area for me and some friends. It didn't make any difference, people just rushed it and, though they meant well, they couldn't see I was suffocating. It was scary.

I'M PROVING YOU CAN GET TO THE TOP AND ENJOY LIFE TOO. I'M THE SAME PERSON I ALWAYS WAS...

It was nearly a fortnight before I could get out of Kingston and back to what I thought would be the tranquillity of Trelawny. I should have known better. There was an incredible welcome waiting back there as well. I'd heard about the motorcades which stretched for miles round the parish when I won the 100 metres and then the 200 metres, and I thought the locals might have done enough celebrating.

But no. This party was for the whole Jamaican Olympic track team, and I wasn't the only local with a gold medal. Veronica Campbell-Brown, who carried our national flag in Beijing, had retained her 200m title from Athens, which was a fantastic achievement too.

We had to go to Sam Sharpe Square in Montego Bay to begin a motorcade where we would be transported to our cars on the back of these trucks. We couldn't even get to the trucks, there were so many people congratulating us. We forced our way through and it must have taken an hour and a half to get to the middle of Falmouth, but I

loved it. This was home. Looking over at the video game shop, where I once spent so much time, I reflected how it wasn't so bad that my cousin had spilled on me to my parents and I'd had to go to training instead of blowing all my dinner money on Nintendo.

It was a few days before everything calmed down, but then at last I was able to relax and walk round Sherwood among people who'd known me since I was a little boy. They were glad to see me and I was pleased to shake their hands and have pictures taken with them. I'm a people person, who enjoys mixing. Other athletes are a little bit more reserved, even my own countryman Asafa. He does everything low key, while I like to live as normal a life as possible.

I know why people love me and appreciate that I make them happy, but it's impossible to please everyone. After the Olympics we were swamped by requests to attend dinners and be presented with awards. I was grateful for all the offers, but I couldn't be everywhere and had to turn a lot down, which I didn't like doing.

One dinner I did attend was the World Athlete of the Year gala in Monaco. It was no surprise to win the award, which was presented by Prince Albert of Monaco, and it was nice to be acknowledged not just as a sprinter but as the best in all of track and field. Oh, and there was a prize of US$100,000 to go with the trophy. One big award I didn't get was the male performance of the year award, which went to Dayron Robles, the Cuban 110m hurdler who broke the world record in the Czech Republic before winning the Olympic gold.

We stayed in the Monte Carlo Casino Hotel, which is the one above the tunnel the grand prix drivers race through, and partied into the night. It was a great end to a great year.

I was supposed to start training a month after the Olympics finished, but Coach generously gave me another three weeks off because I was worn out. It put me behind in my preparations for the 2009 season, which was going to be another big one with the World

Championships taking place in Berlin, and I really had to work hard for three or four weeks to catch up. There was hardly any social life for me, which was almost as painful as the training.

I'd got myself back towards fitness when, at the end of April, I had a crash in my new BMW M3 which could have killed me. How I escaped with no serious injury is a miracle. The car had only been delivered to me in the February as a reward from Puma for my Olympic performances, and I couldn't wait to get it out on the road and burn it up.

On this particular day I was driving along Highway 2000 with two female passengers in the back. It was early afternoon and, with the rain coming down hard, I was going along sensibly, not fast at all. I was driving bare-foot, but I always did that in a car with a gearstick, and I remember changing into third as I slowed down. All I can think is that by leaning my foot to the left I must have accidentally turned off the traction control which had been switched on for the wet. Without any warning, we started skidding across the road and there was absolutely no way of getting the car back under control. The car spun round and we shot backwards, hit the kerb and flew into the air. As we took off I put my hand up to the roof to try and stop me hitting my head and I remember thinking, 'Oh God, we're in trouble, this is gonna hurt.' I can visualise every moment in my mind, and whenever I see a car crash in a film on TV it brings it back to me. In films they are stunts – this was for real. We flipped over and over three times before the car landed with a thud on its roof in a ditch.

For a moment there was silence. Were we dead? No, it seemed not. I crawled out through the side door, but was in a daze as I saw that the car was a total write-off. I'd completely forgotten there were two people in the back but, as soon as I remembered, I went back to the car to help them. One girl was already getting out, but the other was almost unconscious and I couldn't figure out how to open the door to get to her. I was panicking and didn't know what might happen. The car could have been about to blow up. By then another motorist had scrambled down from the highway to help us, and we pulled her clear. The girl's head was bleeding a lot and she had also busted her knee, while the other one had strained her back but was otherwise OK.

WITHOUT ANY WARNING, WE STARTED SKIDDING ACROSS THE ROAD... THE CAR SPUN ROUND AND WE SHOT BACKWARDS...

Ridiculously, having rolled the BMW three times, smashed it to bits and somehow escaped without a bruise or a scratch, I got hurt walking on thorn prickles in the ditch because I had no shoes on. I stepped on the thorns three or four times as I was wrestling with the door to help one of the girls out.

We were taken to hospital in Spanish Town and the doctors tried removing the thorns, but there were quite a number stuck in my foot and they didn't make a great job of it, although I'm most appreciative of all that the doctors did for me that day. If Mom had been there it would have been fine; she used to pull thorns out all the time after I'd been playing in the fields round our house.

But a thorn or two in my foot was a small price to pay. I must be blessed, because everyone in that car could have died. There should be no way you can flip a car like that and come out of it as well as we did.

I don't have flashbacks about it. Yes, car crashes in films bring it back to me, but I don't have nightmares in bed or anything, I'm just thankful I'm still here. I've had three car crashes in my life and this was the worst. I've been very lucky.

The prickles in my foot prevented me from training for almost two weeks, but I decided to go ahead with a special 150m race being held on the streets of Manchester in England. I was keen to do it. I liked the idea of taking athletics to the people in a city centre. All we had to do was lay out a track down the middle of the street and get on with it. My foot was hurting and felt like there was something still sticking into it, so I had to run on it at an angle to stop the pain. It wasn't ideal but I could manage and it made the race more of a challenge.

Coach wasn't sure about me doing it, but I wanted to try. It was something different which helped the profile of athletics and I didn't want to let the organisers down. I like the concept of just turning up and running with no stadium required. You couldn't do it for the javelin or the hammer but you can for a sprint race.

It was a horrible day, with rain pouring down during the heats. I'd been allowed to miss them and just race the final, which fortunately was when the sun came out. The wet weather made the track bouncy and I broke the world record in a time of 14.35 seconds. Though the 150m is not an official distance in our sport, it was good to be back after the crash with no ill effects.

I'd had very little time to prepare because of the accident, but thanks to the enthusiasm from the people of Manchester, who enjoyed the race so much, I was happier than usual. Bring on the World Championships!

SADIKI RUNAKO BOLT

HALF-BROTHER

Usain and I got really close in 2003, when he came into Kingston to live. Before that, I would only visit during a few summer or Christmas holidays in Trelawny. So although we spent very little time together before, it changed once we were in the same city.

I grew up in Kingston with my mom, so I found the rural life a little boring at times, but it could also be refreshing. Of course I would play cricket and football with the other young boys in the neighbourhood.

Usain says he could play cricket and bowl a bit, but I was the real cricketer in the family and am currently playing club cricket for Melbourne Cricket Club in Jamaica – home of the famous West Indian fast bowler, Courtney Walsh.

There's a lot of sporting rivalry between Usain and me, but it's hard to compete with such a talented sprinter. As a junior I tried out for the national cricket squad, without much luck. I was out early at the under-15 trials and broke my favourite bat. I had made lots of runs playing for Calabar High School, which helped me to go into senior league cricket.

I therefore have to be content with fighting it out on the FIFA soccer video game with Usain. At least I can beat him at that. We've always got on and never really had any major arguments. We like watching football together too; we're both Manchester United fans.

I only realised how good an athlete he was when he won the 200 metres at the world juniors in Kingston. I was like, shocked, when he ran that crazy time at the age of 15. The whole of Jamaica was celebrating with Usain.

I didn't go to the Beijing Olympics but saw it on television with my friends, and one of them was beating the door so hard when Usain won the 100 metres, I thought he was going to put his fist through it. It was a phenomenal feeling to know that was my brother.

I did get the glorious opportunity to attend the World Championships in Berlin. It was fantastic to be there to see him repeat his victories in both events at the World Championships. It felt like I was living part of it.

There's a certain glory in being Usain's brother, and I admit I've used it from time to time with the girls. If I'm out clubbing with him, it certainly helps with the opposite sex. I am more of the smooth, handsome type and am definitely leading him in that department. At least I am sure I am beating him at something.

CHAPTER 10

BERLIN AND BEYOND

BERLIN WAS WHERE I WAS GOING TO continue towards my status as an athletics great. Could I do it all over again a year after the Olympics? Of course I could.

First there were the Jamaican trials to go through. There were no exemptions, even for an Olympic champion and world record holder. I had to earn my place on the team all over again, and I won the 100 and 200 metres comfortably.

At my English training camp at Brunel University I asked Coach for a 400m training programme to boost my strength. I'd run a couple of 400m races and worked with my friend Jermaine Gonzales, who is a specialist 400m man. We did a series of 150m runs, where you had to do each one in around 17 seconds and, after a minute's rest, go again. After eight 150s the programme was finished, and when I'd done it, I knew I was ready.

Tyson Gay was making noises about beating my 100m world record after running the fastest time of the season in 9.77 in Rome. I wasn't worried. I'd done a 200 metres a few days earlier in Lausanne, clocking 19.59 on an awful rainy night, and didn't push all the way to the line. It was one hundredth outside Tyson's best 200m of the year. A week later, in Paris, for my first Golden League meeting of the season I posted 9.79 in the 100m without any trouble. I knew how to beat him. Whatever he ran I could run faster.

We avoided each other before Berlin, but on arrival in Germany I felt the same way as before the Olympics – I was going to win another three gold medals. I also thought the 100m and 200m world records would go again, because there was Tyson and Asafa in the 100 and Tyson in the 200. After what happened at the Olympics, Tyson was not going to Berlin for a silver. He wanted to stop me being the number one athlete in the world. But I was tuned in to winning, even if it was going to take another world record to do it. I wasn't going to be repeating Beijing by shutting down in the final 15 metres, though. I didn't think that would be possible this time round. I might be the best, but the others were no mugs. They were seriously fast guys who were capable of taking advantage of any mistakes.

The 100m heats were on day one around lunchtime, and I breezed it, as did Tyson. Then came the quarter-finals that evening, where my training partner Daniel Bailey was in the lane to my left. We got away together and were joking with one another as we jogged over the line and qualified as first and second. Again I got criticism for fooling about like at the Olympics, but it was funny for Daniel to be there beside me showing that if I could jog and qualify, he could too. He even edged me out by one hundredth of a second. Meanwhile Tyson and Asafa were winners in their respective races.

> ## I POPPED THE BLOCKS A FRACTION TOO EARLY, AND YOU COULD HEAR THE SHOCK AND THE 'OOOOOHS' ALL ROUND THE STADIUM.

The semi-finals caused a stir when I false-started after me and Daniel had a bet about who could get away quickest. I popped the blocks a fraction too early, and you could hear the shock and the 'oooooohs' all round the stadium. I thought, 'Calm down, people.' There are pictures of me smiling after the false start and it's because I'd almost got it right and done Daniel, while he was laughing about me going early.

The next time we went the gun again sounded for a false start and the cameras zoomed in, everyone wondering if it was me. If so I was out, which would have been a very big deal – but it wasn't me. Unfortunately for the British athlete Tyrone Edgar, it turned out to be him and he was disqualified. I made no mistake when we got away the third time and did a 9.89, to Tyson's 9.93 in the other semi.

The final was just over two hours later, and I had a bet with my masseur Eddie and my agent Ricky where we each put in 100 euros

and guessed my time. Whoever got closest would take the 300 euro pot. I said I'd do 9.54, Eddie 9.57 and Ricky an unbelievable 9.5. My world record from Beijing was 9.69 and, good though I was, Ricky was taking it too far. I chatted with Daniel as we waited, and we started messing around doing dances and stuff, while Tyson was looking at us as if to say, 'What are they doing?'

As you line up for a race the camera comes really close, and Daniel in lane three was sort of doing punches towards the lens. When it came to me in the next lane, I was jumping around telling the audience to enjoy the race, and even Asafa got into it, chewing up his number. Tyson, in lane five, wasn't having any of it; a salute to the crowd was all.

The stadium was full, the atmosphere electric. I took a deep breath and settled on my blocks. 'On your marks, set...' and we were off. In two strides I'd got the jump on Tyson and was ahead of him. Coming up out of the drive phase I could feel him on my shoulder, but he wasn't in my direct eye line and I was pulling away. With ten metres left I'd got it, but what was the time going to be? Who was going to win the 300 euros? As I glanced at the clock I wasn't looking to see if it was a world record, I knew that was going to go, I wanted to know who'd won the money. Wow, 9.58 – it was Eddie's. Oh well, good for him, I'd have to make do with a gold medal and a world record.

To my astonishment, as I kept running round the corner there was a photographer carrying a heavy, long-lens camera, and not the leanest man you'll ever see, who was absolutely belting along to keep up with me and get his pictures. If he'd been in the final he might have had a chance.

There were thousands of Jamaicans in Berlin, many of whom had foam Bolt arms which they strapped over their shoulders. I did my Bolt 'To the World' signature, which by now was far more refined than in Beijing. Then I hooked up with Asafa, who had taken bronze behind Tyson, and we did a little dance together. Asafa was learning to loosen up at last!

I went over to the clock for the now regulation shot of me beside the world record time and heard that Tyson had run 9.71, which was only two hundredths off my old world best. But, as I said, no matter how well he ran I was confident I would always go better.

In training I could never post a time like that. Against my team-mates at the Racers Track Club my fastest would be around 10.7, but there is a different mindset when it comes to competition.

Tyson withdrew from the 200 metres, apparently with a groin injury, which was a shame. There were claims in the media that he was avoiding me. I don't know the truth of it, but he wouldn't have beaten me anyway.

I won my heat, the quarter-final and the semi, while Wallace was first home in the other semi in a pretty good time. I wasn't thinking about losing, just whether I could set another world record. The TV interviewers were telling me it could be done, but I imagined it was going to be tight, coming down to a couple of hundredths at the most.

My game plan was to go out hard, keep my form round the corner and give it everything down the straight. My reaction time was the best of all the finalists, which was a rarity, and as I got going and came off the bend the bright numbers on the clock were showing something like 14 seconds. I'd never seen that before at this stage of the race and wondered if the timer was working properly. Usually it would be showing 15 or moving on to 16. I kept driving on and was going to lean forward at the tape but decided it wasn't necessary. I was going to break the record, it was only a question of by how much. The time showed as 19.2 but was rounded down to 19.19. As with the 100 metres, I'd beaten my previous mark by 11 hundredths, which was a strange coincidence.

I lay flat on the ground and needed the help of the games mascot, Berlino the Bear, to get me up. This was one clever bear and he stopped me to do the 'To the World' sign with him. The photographers missed it

and we had to go through the routine again for them before Berlino ran 50 metres down the track with me. Had there been a world bears race I'm sure he would have won. Berlino versus the photographer would have been an interesting contest.

I was pleased Wallace got a bronze medal for the second successive World Championships. He had lost bronze at the Olympics when he was disqualified for stepping out of his lane. It was some reward for him after a season troubled by injuries.

Two gold medals down, one to go. I'd like to say I was up for the 4x100m relay and another world record, but I wasn't. I was shattered, far more than in Beijing.

If my third leg in China was ordinary, this was worse. There was no life in me. Somehow I got the baton round to Asafa, but did nothing to help the team. I just carried the thing round and handed it on. We were more than two tenths down on Beijing but well clear of Trinidad and Tobago, who were second. If the 4x100 metres was run at the start of the games we would obliterate the record, but that would affect my 200m performance, so you cannot have everything.

Mike Powell, the holder of the world long jump record, which has stood at 8.95 metres since 1991, was interviewed while we were in Berlin. He thought I could be the first to leap nine metres if I took up the event. 'I can show Usain how to jump nine metres,' he said. 'For a small fee! With his height he is the type who would scare me. We are dealing with a freak of nature athlete. He is off the charts. He is destroying other athletes, making them look like kids.'

Those words made me think, and I've told Glen Mills I want to try long jump before retiring, but it's not in my immediate plans. I've had a go at Racers Club on a training night and done two or three during the warm-up at track meets, registering about 6.90 with a half run-up.

I don't know how much specialised coaching would be needed. There is a certain amount of technique required with the way you distribute your weight and get your feet in the right position. And how fast should I approach the pit? If I went flat out it would be hard to hit the board at the right point, so I would have to go at about 75 per cent, which would lose me some of my advantage. That's for the future, and I'm sure Coach will have me doing 400s before getting to long jump.

Missing the world record in the relays didn't take the edge off the championships for me. I'd done what I set out to do and was ready to celebrate. It didn't turn out the way I planned, though, because I had to DJ for the whole night. I fancy myself as a part-time DJ and asked the guy on stage at this club in Berlin to move over. He was playing a load of rubbish and we needed to get the place going. When I'd done about an hour and was ready to let him have his decks back, he'd disappeared. Not only had he left the stage, he'd left the club, and there was no one else except me to do the job. I was up there for five hours and sweated buckets. I almost ran out of songs and was playing all kinds of crap. I couldn't go on any longer and announced over the microphone, 'People, it's time to go home' – and we did.

One of my rewards for my efforts in Germany was a piece of the Berlin Wall. I assumed I'd be able to take it straight home, but it turned out to be 12 feet high and weighed about two tonnes, with a big picture of me painted on the side. At least I think it was me, because as I stood there accepting this historic piece of concrete from the Mayor of Berlin I couldn't help looking at it and thinking, 'That doesn't look anything like me.' The clue was that the figure was black and in a Jamaican running vest, but apart from that it could have been anyone.

I said all the right things about how being given something of such significance was a great honour, but I didn't know what I was going to do with it. They shipped it back to Jamaica and I thought of putting it out at the front of my new house, but I couldn't get over the fact that the picture was dreadful, so I scrapped the idea. It is now sitting in an army camp. I'd scrape the painting off, but I've been told that would be disrespectful.

A sponsor also gave me a 400m running track. It was a proper eight-lane blue track, worth about US$350,000 and something we really needed at the university where we train. It was transported over in huge containers and will be put to very good use.

The reaction to my performances in Berlin was nothing like as crazy as after the Olympics. I got a fantastic reception at my next meeting in Zurich and was mobbed at the train station, but it was a lot less crazy. It was never going to be the same, even having set two new world records.

Asafa almost got me in the 100 metres in Zurich, where the starter is one of the faster ones. When the gun went I was still in the blocks and caught him 30 metres from home. It was a close one.

Asafa and I understand each other. We are competitors, and he's a good athlete and a former world record holder who I looked up to when I was coming through. He's been very consistent and has the record of most sub tens in track and field. I won't ever match that, because I run 100 and 200 metres whereas he only does 100. But I've worn him down now. This is my time.

I finished the year off in Brussels with a 200 metres, beating Wallace into second place. It had been a hard season and a very rewarding one. I didn't want another big fuss when I returned to Jamaica, and booked my ticket at the last minute without telling anyone, so there were no motorcades waiting. I couldn't have done that again, and probably neither could the police – once was enough.

I retained the athlete of the year title in Monaco and told the audience how I'd refocused after the car crash and put in a lot of hard work. The president of the IAAF, Lamine Diack, said I'd raised my performances to 'an unimaginable level', adding, 'We need stars. Usain Bolt is one of the best known people on the planet and brings a lot of prestige to our sport.'

In the winter I moved into my new house, losing my world championship medals in the process. I was sure Mr Peart had them, and he thinks they were with me, but they haven't reappeared although we've looked everywhere we can think of. Hopefully they will turn up one day.

I nearly lost my Olympic medals as well when we were in New York. They were in a bag which I left in one of the guest rooms, then forgot where I'd put it. We searched all over my room and round the hotel for hours before finding them.

While I was pleased to get them back, I've won hundreds since I was at school. It's special when you win your first one, but after a while the novelty wears off. It's not the piece of metal that matters, it's the achievement itself. I don't need to see the medals to know I won, and I don't have to show them to anyone to prove it. Everybody knows.

" I NEARLY LOST MY OLYMPIC MEDALS AS WELL WHEN WE WERE IN NEW YORK. THEY WERE IN A BAG WHICH I LEFT IN ONE OF THE GUEST ROOMS..."

AUNTY LILLY

Usain was an active child from the moment he was born, more than any other child I've ever seen. I remember his father, my younger brother Gideon, coming to see me all worried saying, 'Miss Lilly, there's something wrong with VJ, he's not normal. He keeps flipping over and jumping, and when he goes into the kitchen to fetch something for his mum he never walks, he always runs.'

I told Gideon there was nothing wrong with the boy. He wouldn't listen to me, he was sure it wasn't normal behaviour. The doctor finally convinced him Usain was just an energetic child and there was nothing to be bothered about.

Usain would come to my house after school, and I'd sit on the veranda watching him coming towards me with that walk of his, and say to myself, 'Wow, that boy is dun cyah,' which is patois for 'don't care'. Nothing worried him. He was going to be alright in the world.

Usain would give me a big hug and say, 'Aunty Lilly, you nuh cook yet?' and I'd have to get him his pork to eat before he went home for another meal. His mother wouldn't cook pork because of her religion, she is Seventh Day Adventist, but he knew he'd get it at my house. He loved pork with dumplings and hated fish. He'd never eat it.

Having a farm and a shop next door to the house, I've always been the one who feeds the big family gatherings. I don't mind, that's how it works in Jamaica, and it's lovely to have the family aroun'. We've been thinking about a full-scale reunion, but it would be hard to organise and finding a date would be almost impossible. If we could do it, it would be great.

On Saturdays Usain came over with his dad, and Gideon would run the shop for me while I went off to the market to sell the yam I harvested from the farm. Before I went Usain would ask if I could 'make up' and give him some money, so he could buy biscuits and sweets from the shop. Even now when he's back from Kingston he will come and say, 'Aunty Lilly, can I have two sweeties, just two?'

At Christmas, after the World Championships, Usain was at my house eating his meal as usual in the kitchen. We don't tell anyone when he's here, yet somehow the word gets out and the kids come round to see him. I don't know how he deals with his life now. It must be strange getting so much attention for a boy who grew up in the quiet of the country. It hasn't changed him, not at all. He's the same VJ from childhood, loving and giving, who says 'good morning' or 'good evening' to everyone.

I have lots of his cuttings from the newspapers, some in scrapbooks and some in frames on my wall. One of his favourite pictures on the wall is of him showing his muscles at a training session before Beijing. He always says, 'Look at those muscles.'

We are an open house. I get the media coming round and I've come to enjoy doing the interviews. Being a minor celebrity is good for business too. During the Olympics two American tourists turned up and watched the 100 metres in the house with us. They thought it was great to be able to watch Usain win the gold while sitting with his aunty.

I had total confidence in him at the start of that race. I wasn't nervous, but I wanted to scream for ever when he won. I ran outside waving my Jamaican flags, and everyone for miles around came out. We are a quiet community, but it wasn't that night. I started a motorcade from my house and we blocked roads for miles.

I've only seen Usain's races on television, but I hope to be able to see him compete at the London Olympics in 2012. Perhaps we could get all the family over and have our big reunion there.

CHAPTER 11
MY ISLAND
IN THE SUN

IF THERE WERE GOLD MEDALS FOR PARTYING I'd have won every year from 2003, when I moved to Kingston at the age of 17, until I was 20. On a good night out when the vibes were right I would have a couple of bottles of Guinness and still go off to training the next day.

For a country boy the attractions of the big city were irresistible. Dad had kept me on a very tight rein, hardly ever letting me go out, and on the rare occasions he did, he slapped down such an early curfew that I was supposed to be home long before the fun started. When I didn't stick to the rules I would be punished for it. In Kingston I could do whatever I wanted – freedom!

I maintain that the reason my athletics career stalled around those same years was down to injury, not my lifestyle, but I probably did go too far and gave the critics a convenient stick to beat me with.

I have no regrets – it made me who I am. I have to relax and enjoy life to get the best out of myself. If I did everything by the book I'd be a very dull boy and I'm sure it would have a negative effect on my running.

Guinness is an Irish drink but it is also big in Jamaica. Rumour has it that when Bono from the band U2 came over and tried it, he said it was the best Guinness he'd ever had. It supposedly does you good because of the nutrients, so I had plenty, to be sure of getting as much goodness as possible.

There is a well-known song in Jamaica called 'Red Bull and Guinness', recorded by Delly Ranx and Chino, as well as various other artists, which explains the benefits of the two drinks together. Guinness sales went mental when that came out – it was a marketing man's dream. The lyrics are quite explicit, but you would have to know your patois to really get them.

My nights out would not start till 1am and finished at 6am. When you're a young man, enjoying life, you don't worry about it. As I said, I'm a blessed child who was given an amazing talent.

I'm not a trendsetter but I like to look sharp when I go out, usually in black and wearing a nice fly shirt with the long sleeves rolled up. I don't really have a style – I dress how I feel. I enjoy meeting nice women and dancing, but there are nights when I might pop into a club for an hour to see the DJs and go into their booth to pick up a few tips.

I have some DJ decks at home and have played a few clubs in Miami as well as that rather longer than planned set in Berlin. Being a DJ is not easy for a Jamaican, because we want to make sure it sounds smooth and you can't just switch from one song to the other. Every song has a certain beat, like 93, 95 or 97, and you have to set the tempos. Hip-hop is really hard to work with, because you are playing with beats of 125 or 126 and it's all over the place. I admire the guys who do it well – it takes a lot of practice.

Jamaica is famous for its reggae, and Bob Marley is the King of Reggae. Every kid grows up on him even today, and you still hear Marley mixes in the clubs. But music has developed from what Marley did and gone in different directions. I used to like hip-hop when I was at school and would borrow CDs and cassettes off my class-mates. I never had any of my own, as Dad thought they were one of those unnecessary expenses which weren't essential to life. I couldn't load tracks on to an iPod because we didn't have iPods back then.

Dancehall is my favourite music. It started in the late '70s as a form of reggae, but has changed a lot over the years with the use of huge sound systems and digital technology made popular by the likes of Bounty Killer and Beenie Man. It gets criticised for its violent lyrics, which have led to fights between rival gangs and eventually a crackdown by the Government. I don't listen too much to the words, I like it simply because it is music you can dance to.

I'M NOT A TRENDSETTER BUT I LIKE TO LOOK SHARP WHEN I GO OUT

The authorities didn't see it like that, which was why our 9.58 Superparty celebration, which we organised in the December after Berlin, was suddenly closed down by the police. The idea was to raise money for the health centre in Sherwood and to get some top acts along too. Wallace and Asafa came, and the American rapper Ludacris flew in. The vibes were good and we were having a lot of fun, apart from when Wallace started saying I couldn't dance. I think I'm really good. The main act of the night was Vybz Kartel, one of my favourite DJs. For the police that was all the information they needed to stop the fun.

You have to understand the recent history of the Jamaican music scene to know why the police thought it necessary to take such heavy-handed action. Over a period of four years two factions had sprung up called Gaza and Gully. Vybz Kartel was from Gaza, which identified with the town of Portmore where he came from. Another top DJ called Mavado was Gully, which referred to the place he was born, Cassava Piece in St Andrew, where there was a line of shacks along a stretch of gullies. Music fans would take one side or the other and there was a lot of fighting in schools and clubs. You couldn't like both sides, at least not publicly.

I never felt it was the artists' fault, more their followers', but maybe that's because I didn't think too deeply about the lyrics. I was Gaza, although that didn't mean I didn't like people who were Gully. Bounty Killer was Gully and we would still talk together.

The Prime Minister called dancehall 'verbal nonsense' and said Gaza and Gully were 'one example of the negative influences that destabilise us as a people and destroy our confidence in ourselves'. The Government decided the only answer was to start closing shows down, and shutting my party was the best way to get their new hard-line message across.

With everything going great at the Superparty and Vybz about to come on stage at 4am, the police stormed into the marquee and literally pulled the plugs out. They said we were disturbing the neighbours, although we were in the middle of a field. It was just an excuse and I was so annoyed about it. Vybz was the act everyone had come to see, and he couldn't go on. The police officer was acting all bossy and rough, telling us the show was over, and I was saying to him, 'What's all that about?' He wouldn't listen. I wanted to get on to the Prime Minister and the head of police right then, and didn't care about getting them out of bed. Vybz – hardly a man of violence – told me to leave it alone.

Two days later Vybz and Mavado had a peace meeting with the Prime Minister and called for the Gaza and Gully battle to end. Mavado said, 'I never threw a stone at Vybz and he never did it to me. It is just about music, but we have fans out there and people take it to a different level, so me and Vybz have to talk to these fans and do things to mend the situation.' Vybz agreed, saying, 'People need to realise that there has never been any personal animosity.

Sometimes people take things out of context, especially impression-able minds.'

That was the end of Gaza and Gully, and it all came to a head at my party. Maybe it was for the best; perhaps the violence had got out of control. But the rivalry had made for some great shows like the Sting Festival, billed 'the greatest one-night reggae show on earth', where you would get both Gaza and Gully artists on stage trying to outdo each other in a lyrics war. Whenever one rapper stumbled over his words he would get it from the crowd, and the winner would be decided by the reaction he generated. Admittedly it did spill over into violence sometimes, but now it's gone the other way. The show in December 2009 after the peace meeting with the Prime Minister was the most boring thing ever.

You have to be Jamaican to get Jamaica. The way we act, the way we live and the way we speak is like nowhere else. If I'd written this book in Jamaican patois, or creole as the linguists call it, most of you wouldn't have understood a word of it. It is not meant to be written down, but it is how many kids and adults speak to one another on the island. We drop letters from the English language and run words together and, while we grow up on it, it's very difficult to follow for a foreigner. It's so specialised that even in neighbouring Caribbean islands like Barbados or Trinidad they cannot understand us. They have their own forms of it, which are different from ours.

When I moved to Kingston and started running professionally I had to take special English lessons so that in interviews people would know what I was saying. I had problems with words like three, which I would say as 'tree'. I couldn't work out that you had to roll the words off your tongue. The teacher showed me how to set my tongue to say

"JAMAICA IS THE TYPE OF SOCIETY WHERE EVERYTHING CAN BE DONE TOMORROW"

the word properly. I can adapt now, according to who I'm speaking to, but with friends and family we always use patois. Some native Jamaicans cannot speak proper English at all, they talk patois all the time – and it's raw patois. When I'm talking to my mom a normal English-speaking person could probably pick up some words, but raw patois is impossible – you would have no chance.

Jamaica is the type of society where everything can be done tomorrow, and I'm as guilty as the rest. I'll wake up and think that I have to do two things, then decide, 'No, forget it, I'll do it tomorrow.' Tomorrow comes and you think, 'No, the next day' – until there comes a point where you have to do it, and you do it.

I love the place and the people, even though they gave me a lot of grief when I was younger. They will support you 150 per cent, and when the Olympics or World Championships are on, the whole country comes together. Jamaica has a reputation for violent crime but there is none when there is a big sports event on, because everyone is watching TV. Once it's over, normal life resumes.

I want us to have a better society, and I try to help kids so they don't have to go down that path. For some it's inevitable but for most it's avoidable and we can help them before they reach adulthood. If you can show kids the right way to go, the way to work hard and the way to be focused, there will be less poverty.

CHAPTER 12
OFF THE
TRACK

MY BEST FRIEND IN THE WORLD IS still NJ, or Nugent Walker junior. We have been friends ever since we met on the first day at Primary School and I can't remember ever falling out with him. We hit it off straight away and now he's my personal assistant, someone I can turn to at any time of day and night, who is always, always there for me. Sometimes you have friends who you are forever cussing and then might not talk to you for a while, but that has never happened with us.

The only thing we ever argued about when we were growing up was maths, because we were both good at it and would fight over the best way to solve a problem. He was more into his schoolwork than sport – although we played in the cricket team together – as we went from Primary and on to William Knibb High School.

Throughout the bad times, when I was trying to get over injuries and the Jamaican public were criticising me, NJ was on the end of a phone to talk to. If he heard things were not going well, he would call

and ask what the problem was and between us we'd come up with the best way to go forward and deal with it. During the Olympics and World Championships I could ring him no matter what the time difference and he was happy to talk, even if I'd woken him up.

When I moved to Kingston I wanted NJ to come and share a flat, but he had a job at the airport and was getting a place at college. He also thought that if we were together we'd probably get into too much trouble. After college he wanted to go on to do a business degree, but couldn't get on the course, so he's come to work for me while he's waiting for a place. I'm kind of lazy, and NJ does everything I need, allowing me to get on with being an athlete. When the helper doesn't come to work, NJ cooks when I get in and deals with all the day-to-day stuff. While Mr Peart manages me, NJ is the man on the ground. He is the link to the rest of the management team, which now includes a full group – manager, coach, agent, finance director, masseur and publicist.

When I'm asleep, people can call NJ to sort things out, and he can go through it with me when I get up, instead of having people trying to call me 40 or 50 times and not getting a reply.

NJ, Sadiki and I live in my new house in Kingston, which I bought at the start of 2010. It's a place where me and my closest friends, the ones I really trust, can relax. These aren't hangers-on who want to be associated with me because I'm the world's fastest man, they are proper friends. Courtney Walsh junior, the son of the former West Indies fast bowler, often comes over with Jermaine Gonzales. I've known Jermaine since I was 14 and we competed in the world juniors together, where he won a bronze in the 400 metres. We also lived together when we were both at the High Performance Centre in Kingston. We are both big football fans – I'm Manchester United, he's Arsenal. Jermaine has been unlucky with injury, and I also felt he spent too long working with Fitz Coleman before I eventually persuaded him to join me at Racers Track Club. Hopefully he will benefit from that.

My friends and I will watch sports on TV, play video games, and have our big dominoes nights – one of my favourite ways to spend an evening before we go out clubbing.

Many Jamaicans enjoy dominoes and become quite obsessed by it. To some it's just a bar game of chance, where you get the dominoes you pick and it depends on what others play as to whether you can put your own domino down. But it's a very technical game, with a lot of skill involved, especially if you play it in pairs.

There are 28 dominoes in a set, and seven of everything from double blank up to double six, so you have to learn to read people's hands and think about what they have. It's not just about matching the other domino, there's a lot more to it than that.

The art of the game is to find a way not to let the others win, so that you can win. I sometimes think I've got everything figured out, but then I play against guys who've been round dominoes tables for years and they are on another level. Coach Mills is very good, and if he plays with a partner who knows the game too, it's over – there's no point even playing against them. I got really good when I played regularly with Courtney Walsh and the reggae singer Beres Hammond, who are real experts. My friends are not in the same league as them, and don't read the game properly, which can make for some unpredictable contests.

I never get bored with dominoes. I can play for six hours, no problem, and once did it for eight hours from 8pm until 4am without a break. The neighbours must have been pissed about that, we were screaming and cussing. We were playing six-love, in which the aim is to win six straight games in a row. If you do that you get a point, and we play best of three, which is why it can take a long time. The slam of the domino on the table at the point of victory is the fun of it, as you send all the other dominoes flying off the table.

We spend a lot of time on the video games too, and I'm well known down at the local video store. They ring me up as soon as a new game comes in so I can get it straight away. We are into all the popular ones like FIFA Football, Grand Theft Auto and the war game Call of Duty. You can go online, make up a player name and battle it out against gamers all over the world. There are many people who have played against me without realising it. Perhaps one day there will be a Usain Bolt athletics game.

Every Sunday when I'm in Kingston we get a football match going up at the UWI pitch. There's no special protection for me, like a no-tackling rule, it's proper competitive. It wouldn't be fair otherwise. You get roughed up, you fall over, whatever, but I don't worry about getting hurt. You can't close yourself off from everything and stay in all day.

I try not to get found out by Coach, though, because he wouldn't be happy about me playing. He came past me one Sunday when I was going to football, but I kept my window wound up. It's tinted so he couldn't see me, even though he knew it was my car. When we met up at training the following day he said, 'I saw you going to play football.' I replied, 'Me, Coach? Other people drive my van, you know. Are you sure it was me? What was I wearing?' He couldn't answer that. We both knew he knew, but he couldn't prove it.

I'M NOT A CONVENTIONAL ATHLETE. I DON'T FOLLOW ANY OF THE RULES

I'm not a conventional athlete. I do what I like, stay up till whatever time I feel like, socialise when I like and eat what I like. I don't follow any of the rules. For instance, if you asked me what the best food for an athlete is you would be asking the wrong person, and I don't know anything about the correct balance between carbohydrates and protein. I don't have a nutritionist like a lot of other top sportsman, who have all these charts and are told what to eat at different hours of the day. They would have been horrified by my diet of chicken nuggets throughout the Olympics, but it worked for me.

Coach goes on about the benefits of pasta – it digests quickly and you can go out training with more energy. I used to eat it to keep him happy, but I don't bother so much any more, as it doesn't fill you up and two hours later you are hungry again.

I'm aware the weight piles on as you get older if you don't eat the right foods, so I might start taking more notice in a few years' time. If you train as we do, I don't think you need be concerned about a diet. You go to the gym, work on your abs, train down at the track and it all burns off. Eat what you want while you can, I say.

We have a traditional Jamaican dish called Ackee – which is a fruit – and saltfish, which I eat for breakfast. It's supposedly very good for you, but you have to know what you're doing. If it's not prepared and cooked correctly it's poisonous!

My favourite food is pork, preferably from Aunty Lilly, accompanied by anything like dumplings, banana and yam – which is like sweet potato. On a Sunday I'll have what everyone else in Jamaica has, chicken, rice and peas. Away from the home-cooked specialities the hot wings from Kentucky Fried Chicken are to die for. God, I just love them, cannot get enough. I would happily eat a fry-up too, if it's put in front of me. The only thing I'm not keen on is onions – not because of the taste, it's the crunching sound they make. When Mom does onions with rice, she cooks the onions up big so I can pick them out.

Apart from my love of food, video games, football, and partying, I'm also into cars, fast ones. When we were growing up every teenager wanted a Honda. You could soup them up in different ways, spray-paint them, put turbos on them and, because everyone had one, there were plenty of garages to do the job with all the parts available. These days one of my dreams is to own a Lamborghini. It would be pointless in Jamaica though, as there's no garage to service it. If it ever broke down you'd be stuck.

My first car was a Honda Accord, which I wrecked in three weeks. I was about to turn off the road to check out a young lady at TGI Friday's and stopped to wait for the traffic on the other side to clear. A guy flashed me to let me go, but a car on the inside kept going and crashed full speed into me. There was a massive impact as he smashed through the left-hand door, but fortunately in Jamaica we are right-hand drive.

I freaked out at first and tried to get out through the window of the door which had been hit rather than simply opening the door on the driver's side. I got a cut on the side of my face but otherwise I was unhurt.

It took a while sorting out the insurance and it was six months before I got a replacement Honda Torneo, which survived undamaged for a year. That was until one morning at the start of the year when I decided I was going to be good and disciplined and go to the gym before training. This guy came out of a side-road into the left-hand lane with me outside him accelerating past. He didn't look and drifted across into my lane. I honked the horn but he kept on coming. With nowhere else to go I hit the brakes hard but couldn't stop slamming into the back of him. He got a cracked bumper while my bonnet was pushed in and the radiator busted. I was pissed because the rules of the road say if you hit someone in the back it's your fault no matter how the accident happened. I got that car repaired and still have it today.

Those two crashes were nothing like the third one in which my BMW M3 was totally written off. Having had three big smashes makes me sound like a liability, but on each occasion I've been going slowly and they weren't caused by me doing anything reckless. As you can imagine, though, my insurance premiums are pretty high, especially as I own six cars. Apart from the Honda Torneo, I have a Honda Accord, a BMW 335, a Nissan GTR Skyline, a Toyota Tundra truck, and an Audi Q7, all of them in black, my favourite colour.

The Skyline, which I call my batmobile, is a beautiful sports car which stays in the garage and only comes out for special occasions, while the Tundra truck was a prize for breaking the world record in New York. I didn't get it delivered until nearly two years later and it wasn't as good a deal as it sounds. The truck is worth US$40,000, and I had to pay almost as much again in duties and taxes because there are heavy penalties for having such a big machine in Jamaica. I like it, though, and use it all the time as a runaround while NJ drives the Audi.

I'd like more cars if I had any more drive space to fit them in. If I ever get the Lamborghini I'm going to buy it in the States and leave it in Miami, where I'm planning to buy a three-bed condo. I'm often over there and it's only an hour's flight. My ultimate car is an original 1968 Ford Mustang Shelby, which was one of the cars Nicholas Cage stole in the film *Gone in 60 Seconds*, but I'm going to have to get out and win a few more races to afford one. They are very rare and cost $250,000.

CHAPTER 13

COPING WITH FAME

DANCING IS ONE OF MY GREATEST PASSIONS ... apart from running, of course. I like to dance, but not when I'm outside Jamaica, and it has nothing to do with Wallace Spearmon saying I'm no good.

Being in the spotlight, I too have had my fair share of run-ins with the media. The way people dance in the dance-hall is not necessarily the accepted norm for how individuals should conduct themselves. I was guilty of expressing this art of dancing outside Jamaica and got a lot of criticism – pictures were taken of me and plastered all over the internet.

The world was clearly not impressed, and from that day on I have acted more responsibly, especially when I am outside Jamaica. It's because of an incident in Miami, which was blown out of proportion and taught me that once you become famous little things can get you into big trouble.

This is one of the hazards of fame, but most of the time I'm fine with the attention. I'm a people person and will pose for as many pictures and sign as many autographs as possible. I feel it's my duty to do so. But I can't always keep everyone happy. For example, I remember running through Norman Manley International Airport in Kingston to catch a flight. I had 30 seconds to get on the plane or it was going without me. This lady called out saying, 'Usain, I've got to have your autograph.' I shouted to her, 'Sorry, can't stop,' and she came back at me with 'You'd better stop!' I kept running and made this apologetic face, but she's probably still cussing me today. It was important to her, and the fact I'm telling the story here shows how much it bothered me. I hate letting people down.

If it had happened in the United States, or in London, they would have understood me, because they are used to stars not giving autographs or just signing three or four and moving on. In Jamaica you have to sign everything – if you don't you're the bad guy.

It's impossible for me to hide and disappear into a crowd. Being 6ft 5ins tall, I tend to stand out above others in the street or in the shopping malls. I can walk past someone and see them thinking they recognise me, and even if it takes them a while to realise who it is, they can follow me all the way because I am taller than the average guy. Sometimes I wish I wasn't such a tall guy. But then, would I be such a great sprinter?

Life changed after the Beijing Olympics. I couldn't go anywhere without being surrounded. I got into the clubs a lot easier, though, and was generally treated much better. I didn't feel guilty about getting ahead in lines or getting the VIP treatment. 'I am Olympic champion and a triple world record holder,' I'd say to myself. 'If you can't get special favours after that, when would you get them?'

Previously I'd only been recognised by those who followed track and field, but now everybody knew me across the world. There are occasions when I crave for that old life back again, like when I'm out for a meal with a girl and I'd just like to be left alone. People will wait and wait and wait for an autograph or a picture, but will always come over and ask in the end. Then when you've done it for one, you have to do it for everybody else. They will apologise and say, 'This is the last one' – which makes me laugh. How do they know it's the last one? Do they know everyone in the restaurant?

Sometimes people will accuse me of ignoring them, which puzzles me. They will say I'm getting all hyped up and ask why I don't talk to them. My reply is simply that I don't know them. Think about it: do you talk to everyone you see? How strange would it be if you did?

I'm not complaining, I'm just explaining how it is. Never as a kid did I think about being famous, but I've become one of the most recognisable faces in the world and you have to enjoy it.

You can have fun with it. When I go shopping in a store in the States or Europe and the assistant behind the counter says, 'You look like Usain Bolt,' I'll reply, 'Yeah, I've heard that before.' Then they'll go, 'You know, that guy who's the runner, the fast one,' and I'll say, 'Yeah, I know, but would he be out shopping in this store?' Then they'll say, 'Yeah, you're right, it couldn't be.' It cracks me up every time. You cannot trick kids, though. The moment they say 'You're Usain Bolt' they've got me no matter how much I pretend I'm not. They'll just go, 'Yes, yes, you are,' and you'll hear this big scream of 'Muuuuum! It's Usain Bolt.'

I live as normal an existence as possible. Meet organisers have had to arrange additional security because of the large numbers of spectators. I can assure you that when I attend any public event in Jamaica, security is there for crowd control. I feel I am loved in Jamaica, but as a celebrity you're recommended also to have your own personal security in place.

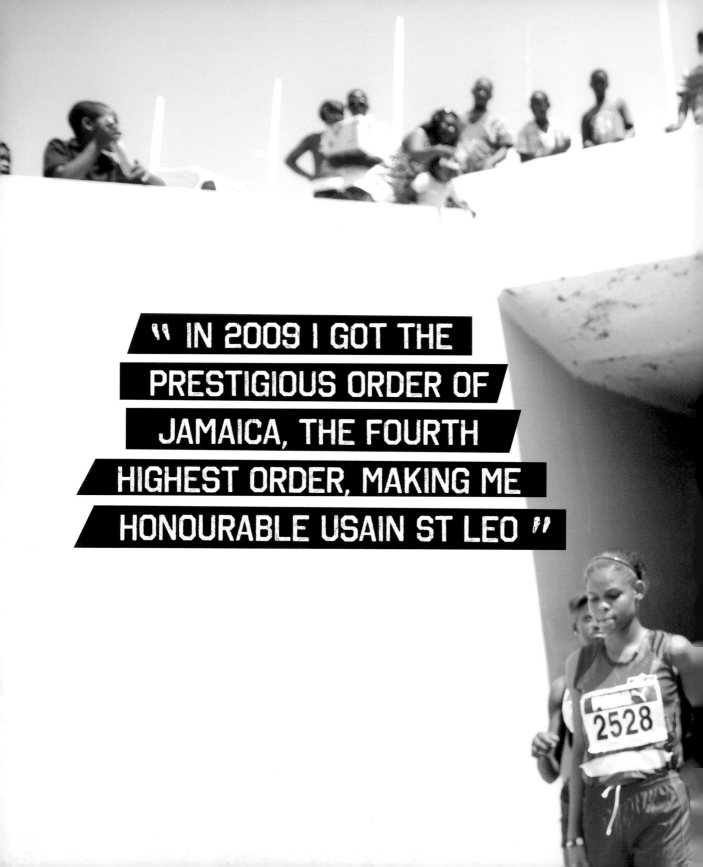

" IN 2009 I GOT THE PRESTIGIOUS ORDER OF JAMAICA, THE FOURTH HIGHEST ORDER, MAKING ME HONOURABLE USAIN ST LEO "

I'm regarded as a role model, which isn't difficult for me to live up to. I'm just being myself, and don't have to work at it. It means setting a good example for kids to follow. On school visits I tell them to work hard so they can achieve whatever they want to, and I don't see my love of the nightlife as a contradiction to that. I'm proving you can get to the top and enjoy life too.

I'm the person I always was – I don't believe success has changed me. When I go to the track to train, my club-mates treat me the same way they always did, they make jokes and we are comfortable in each other's company. They don't think I'm playing the big star, at least I hope not.

I am blessed to be recognised as one of the biggest sports stars, but with this great fame comes even greater scrutiny. I try to live my life as normally as possible, but I am mindful that anything can happen. I follow the news, so I am well aware of what happens with other sporting icons, but I try not to make the same mistakes.

I'M PROVING YOU CAN GET TO THE TOP AND ENJOY LIFE TOO. I'M THE PERSON I ALWAYS WAS...

I have pretty much lived an open life, and my love for having fun is well known. Unlike the USA and Europe, in Jamaica you don't get paparazzi waiting outside nightclubs or your home to get exclusive photos.

I recall being in a club in London after the World Championships. I was pictured leaving with Mickey Rourke, the star of the film *The Wrestler*. He took his shoes off and challenged me to a race down the street. He must be in his mid-50s, but I went along with it – and by the way I did win. I also met the Formula One champion Lewis Hamilton, and David Haye, the world boxing champ who went on to beat that enormous Russian guy Nikolay Valuev, who is more than 7ft tall. I told

him, 'You're stupid, man, if you're really going to fight that guy,' but he did it. I don't go out looking for other famous people but I like mixing with them and talking about their lives when the chance crops up. I did the David Letterman chat show in the US after the Olympics, which was my first big interview appearance. I'd seen his shows before and thought I'd be OK. My personality helped me to play along with his jokes.

My fame gives me an opportunity to help those who are less fortunate and assist other charitable agencies. I also help to influence others to do the same.

I have been involved in a number of projects and am currently working on some others. These have included work in the health, education, community development and sports sectors. We've been working on refurbishing a health centre in my hometown, Sherwood Content, Trelawny. We are also discussing a recreational and play facility

for the same community. Meanwhile from time to time I donate gear for a number of sporting teams.

My sponsors, Digicel, the phone company, helped provide my former primary school, Piedmont Basic School, with a new tiled floor. It might not sound much, but when you've been used to walking around on concrete, it feels a lot more comfortable to walk on tiles.

I hope my fame can help me in achieving one of my greatest ambitions, which is to acquire piped water for my community. The water supply now comes from collecting rain in huge tanks. That works fine, unless it stops raining for a while, in which case water has to be brought in by tanker, which takes a few days. My contribution helps to ensure that the computer lab and the instructor's fees are covered. To me technology is one of the most important subjects for kids.

Not everything I've been involved in has been confined to Jamaica. In

January 2010 Haiti suffered its terrible earthquake, which killed almost 250,000 people. Haiti is only about 300 miles from us and was one of the poorest countries to live in before the 'quake, never mind afterwards. We sent them cases of water and clothes, and I feel there is an obligation on people like me to help out countries hit by natural disasters wherever they are in the world.

I am now a part of the tradition in which the Jamaican Government honours the country's top performing athletes. In 2009 I got the prestigious Order of Jamaica, the fourth highest order, making me Honourable Usain St Leo Bolt. I have followed in the footsteps of numerous other Jamaican athletes who have received national awards dating back to the 1950s. This means I'm an official ambassador of Jamaica with full diplomatic status, and that wherever I am in the world I am representing the country, but then I feel I've been doing that anyway as an athlete since the age of 15.

There was some opposition to the award and a feeling that I was too young for the honour. Most people don't get it until much later in life, Bob Marley received an award after his death. However, I'm proud of it and will use it to help make life better for our people and our sportsmen and women. It gives me easier access to our Prime Minister, and I'm able to raise issues with him which I believe need looking at, such as a better support system for our athletes. I feel track and field have helped to make Jamaica far more popular, and I am sure the rest of the athletes would agree with me.

Jamaica is a popular destination and I was a part of the international media campaign for the Jamaica Tourist Board, which gave me an opportunity to know my countryside. Jamaica has also become a popular destination for photo shoots and commercials, and in early 2010 I did a few in Jamaica. I feel it is very important to promote the island, and I enjoy doing my bit to bring more visitors to the island, create more jobs and boost the Jamaican economy.

NJ

NUGENT WALKER JUNIOR

We became best friends at the age of six. We always thought it was funny, since he was known as VJ and I was NJ. We were both good at maths and most of the girls in school were brilliant at English. There was always a maths versus English challenge going on about who could get the best marks in their favourite subjects.

I'm from a village called Reserve and had to go past Usain's house to get to school. I'd sit outside and wait for him, and we would walk to Waldensia Primary School together. When we went to William Knibb it was the other way around and he'd come by my house in the local taxi and pick me up.

When we were younger I never thought of him as just a runner, he was good at all sports, particularly cricket. We opened the batting together in the last year of primary school, but he'd been scoring more runs and taking more wickets than me. He was with the team for four years. Usain was an outstanding cricketer from then, making the school team, way before the average player, who would start at grade five. I was on the squad in grade four, but didn't play a match. Usain had been playing matches from grade three, that was how outstanding he was. I don't think that has ever happened at Waldensia since then.

Sports day was a major activity at the school. Usain was always competing in many events. We were in different houses. My team wore yellow and his wore blue. The only win I can boast about was beating him in a maths race. Outside of that he was always the dominant athlete. Usain has always had a strong passion for competing. I remember he once slipped at sports day and cried because he lost. He didn't lose again.

In his first two years at high school he didn't take his running seriously. Kids would be out there training every day, but he would turn up for the race, have a little jog, then go out and win. He'd go off to the games room in Falmouth rather than train, but I didn't go with him, I was concentrating on my school work. He wouldn't even tell me he was going to play video games, because he knew I was the more disciplined one, who would tell him, 'You should be going to training.'

Although Usain would win at school sports and parish level, he got whipped at the Regional level in the first two seasons by Keith Spence. By the third season, VJ realised that some amount of discipline was required and he took it more seriously thereafter. He beat Spence the following year at the Regional Championships and made himself a contender at the national level.

Usain and I would watch numerous sports together and we would strategise about winning. One example was when he was to compete against the defending 400m champion, Jermaine Gonzales. I recall it like just yesterday, sitting in the school library strategising about how we would conquer a previous champion.

In our analysis we knew Usain had great 200 metres speed, and felt it prudent to exploit this ability of his. We decided Usain should run the first 200 metres really fast, to make Jermaine panic and take him out of his rhythm. He would try to catch him and overstretch himself. Turns out he did not even complete the race. Usain and I thought the strategy worked. Jermaine, who is now our very good friend, has gone out of his way to persuade us he had an injury before that race. However, I think it needed more than that to convince us. We feel our strategy worked.

Usain and I still preview his race. The coach may not be happy about this, but we still do it. We are very proud of our record to date.

Usain moved to Kingston before me, but we kept in touch via phone a lot. I came to the city in 2006 to start at Teaching College.

Usain doesn't try to concentrate on running for records, he runs to win. If records come along too, that's a bonus. When Usain ran the 100 metres in Kingston in 2008, some bad things were said about his 9.76 seconds. The critics questioned the legitimacy of the time and asked if the clock was working right. We were happy to shut up the doubters when he set the world 100 metres record with his 9.72 seconds in New York before the Olympics. It was like if you set a record in Jamaica it didn't count, it had to be done in Europe or the States.

The 100 metres continued to be an experience for VJ, and I recall being on the phone with him the night before the 100m semi-final and final in Beijing. We knew Usain had a poor start and that the others would try to exploit that by getting out of the blocks super-quick. Usain said, 'NJ, I've got this, it's cool.' He wanted to talk about other stuff away from athletics, but I felt it was important for him to be focused because he wasn't experienced over the 100 metres and had lost to Asafa Powell in Stockholm in 2008 (before Beijing). At the end of the conversation I had to tell him to go to bed and get some rest. Well, the end result of the 100 metres is there for the world to see.

He's not a big sleeper. In Berlin they were five hours ahead of me, and when I got in at midnight he'd want to talk on the phone.

We dreamed about winning a gold medal in Beijing but in the 200 metres not the 100. The 200 metres will always be the bigger one for Usain, I feel, and to beat Michael Johnson's 19.32 in Beijing was the best feeling. Everyone thought that couldn't be broken. People felt 19.4 was the best Usain could ever do. Now, if he ran 19 seconds flat, I wouldn't be shocked.

I was working in a hotel in Maine, USA, on an overseas programme when the Olympics was on and sneaked into one of the rooms to watch the 100m final. There's not many blacks in Maine, so I stood out a bit as I jumped up and down on the bed. I am sure you can imagine my manager wasn't pleased, and nobody believed Usain was my best friend.

In many ways we're so different. Usain is calm, I'm more aggressive. If there's something wrong I want to deal with it immediately, whereas tomorrow will do for him or even the next day. I'm not the party type that he is either. I'll go out sometimes.

I am like his right-hand man, there to make life easier for him so that he can concentrate on his sprinting. While he's off running, I make sure all his business is taken care of. Before he signs anything he makes sure I've seen it and gone through it. You can now imagine the pressure I am under to ensure that he doesn't sign away his life. I'm happy to be able to share his life with him and, though it's now my job, I've always helped him.

We both love watching sports and support Manchester United, but internationally he goes for Argentina and I'm Brazil. In basketball he backs the Boston Celtics and I'm a Lakers man. I started liking United as Dwight Yorke, who comes from Trinidad and Tobago, played for them, while Usain followed them because he thought Ruud van Nistelrooy was a great goalscorer.

We can't miss a United game on the TV. Once we were in Miami when United lost to Everton and it spoiled the entire day, there was so much cussing done about that result.

Usain admires great sportsmen and women. I tell him he's a legend and a bigger star than all of them, but I don't think he believes it. Sometimes it's hard to get him to realise what a superstar he is. To have a stadium full of 90,000 people singing 'Happy birthday to you', as happened to him in Beijing, he's got to be special.

Everything we ever wanted for Usain is coming to him now, after all the hard times. When people were telling him he was too tall to be a sprinter, I was saying it was rubbish. When Usain thought he might not be able to run because of his back problems, I told him to be positive. I'd read how the body can have a transitional phase as it grows and could adapt to things like his curved spine. I was convinced he'd get through it and he did. For me he is the greatest sportsman that ever lived.

TESTIMONIALS 217

CHAPTER 14

HOT TOPIC

MY PERFORMANCES SINCE 2007 IN OSAKA, Japan, have sparked a lot of interest across the globe. It has been said that I am the saviour of athletics, and that, having proved to be a clean athlete and smashed the world record in the flagship 100 metres, I've given the sport its credibility back. Equally I'm well aware that if there was ever any hint of a drug scandal against me it could finish athletics. I can assure you that won't happen.

I had my first drug test at a track meet in Miami when I was still a few weeks shy of my 17th birthday. Since then I have always had to provide information of my whereabouts each day, so that I'm available for random drug testing at any time.

My attitude towards drugs has always been to stay away from them, whether they be performance enhancing or recreational. In fact I don't even like to take the required supplements, because of my fear that one of them might show up on the banned list. I tried a cigarette when I was 13 years old, but I've never touched one since.

The only supplements I bother with are vitamins, which I've been taking since my teenage years – at least I know they're safe. I won't even risk a cold medicine. I prefer an old Jamaican remedy of honey and lime juice, which always puts me right. Someone should market that, it really does the trick.

However careful I am, and however many times I'm tested – and I've probably been tested more than any other sportsman on the planet since breaking the 100m world record – that is still not enough to satisfy some people, who have doubted my performances.

I am fully aware of all the comments from in and out of the athletics arena, but I am committed to my responsibility as the fastest man on the planet.

Any athlete in the top 20 in the world is subject to random testing from the sport's governing body, and with so many Jamaicans ranked at that level, they are continually being tested, not just by the IAAF but WADA too.

Before the Olympics I was tested four times in a week. I'm tested after every race, and every day I have to tell the authorities where I'm going to be in case they want to do a test. They turn up unannounced at any time of day or night. Even while I was putting together this book, they knocked on my door at 6.30am to do a drug test. You can't say, 'Go away and come back later'; you have to produce a sample when they ask you, and if you can't they will stay there till you do. A missed test is a failed test. Those are the very strict rules which govern the sport.

> I'M TESTED AFTER EVERY RACE, AND EVERY DAY I HAVE TO TELL THE AUTHORITIES WHERE I'M GOING TO BE IN CASE THEY WANT TO DO A TEST.

Athletics has been under a cloud because of recent revelations from past champions. As a result, whenever anyone breaks a world record, one of the first questions seems to be, 'Do you think they are on something?' It takes a while afterwards, maybe two years of being tested and tested, before the world is convinced you're clean.

While the amount of testing I'm subjected to can be inconvenient, I've no problem with it – you get used to it. In fact I'm all for more testing. The testers can form a queue outside my house if they want to, because the more often they test me and other athletes and show that we are clean, the better it is for the sport. It's those who fail tests who make the others look bad. It leads to criticisms of athletics as a whole, and it is hard to turn that feeling around. So I thoroughly support the work of IAAF and WADA to monitor athletes' performances through drug testing.

When I was a youngster I never thought about running for money. It was for fun, and winning was a bonus. It wasn't until after the world juniors and my last year at William Knibb that it became apparent to me that if I took it seriously athletics could be my career. It's a short career, however, and I want to earn as much as I can out of it. I'm not paid on a par with the top football stars, but over the last three years I've done well for myself.

I am very involved in the decisions about my business activities, but I'm confident that I have surrounded myself with a professional team who continue to give me good advice in securing my future after athletics. I'm not one of those who don't know where the money goes. I check my bank statements every month, and if there's something I'm not sure about, I'll ask. I'm meticulous when it comes to contracts too, reading through the important clauses.

These days we get all sorts of offers to endorse companies and their products. My management team handles the proposals and recommends the ones they think are best. We then go on to the next stage, examining the details of each proposal before making a decision.

I have a long-standing sponsorship deal with Digicel, and another with Puma which goes back to high school days. Puma stuck by me when I wasn't doing well, and I am still with them to date.

I endorse the drink Gatorade, and my fridge is always stashed full of those bottles. I have done a series of commercials with them over the years, through which I've met other sporting stars. My success has given me the opportunity to do commercials with my team-mates and even my mom. My career as an athlete has evolved, and because of it I have added several dimensions to my life.

These include associations with other brands, a clothing line and fragrances. We are also delving into the entertainment world with the opening of a restaurant, to be named 'Usain Bolt Tracks & Records'. In 2010 we've been working on developing the Usain Bolt brand. We've designed a logo based on my signature pose, accompanied by the motto 'To the World'.

Big Fish
I got a big fish.
the fish in a pail.
went fast.
and I got wet.
Numbers
1. Writing Tablet.
3. Tim has a —
4. The sun is —
5. I can sit —
6. The bus will —
2. Writing Paper.
No party
Bill

When I made that sign after the Olympic 100 metres in Beijing, I couldn't have dreamed of the impact it would have. It turned out to be a brilliant marketing tool. It has everything – the Bolt shooting down the opposition and the world records, and firing off into the stratosphere.

You can't imagine how many times I've had to do that pose since Beijing. When I returned to Europe to compete after the Olympics, people were going, 'Do your Bolt' – and that's when I realised it was becoming my symbol. The crowds went crazy, they loved it.

For a joke I sometimes tell people that my sponsors only let me do the sign so many times a year – it's the way my contract is structured – and they believe me! They go, 'Do the Bolt, do the Bolt,' and I'm saying, 'Sorry, my management team says I can't today.' Even when I'm old and can't run any more, people will still be asking me to do The Bolt.

Companies are paid thousands to come up with an idea like that, and I just did it out of nowhere. Michael Jordan has a big slam dunk jump as his signature – mine is The Bolt. There aren't many people in the world with a symbol, although it was a bit of a mess when I first did it. I've refined it now by the way I lean, and I've tried to get it straighter. The logo is on my spikes and is featured on a range of training gear and clothes which we've brought out.

I love the idea of having my own range. It's my business and I've had input into everything. I like graphics on my clothes, and samurai cartoons and skulls, so we are working on ways to incorporate those images into the design, while the shoes will have high tops, because that's what I like.

Athletics has given me lots of new opportunities, and I want to make the most of them.

MISS LORNA THORPE

HEAD OF SPORTS,
WILLIAM KNIBB HIGH SCHOOL

Colin Campbell, a sports rep on the Jamaican Teachers Association, first told me about Usain, and when I saw this tall, lanky boy winning the primary school finals I thought to myself, 'We have to have him, we have to get him.' High school sports are very competitive and we're always looking out for new talent. You could see Usain was exceptional, so the headmistress Mrs Margaret Lee arranged a scholarship for him.

Although we are away in the country, far from Kingston, there is a proud tradition of producing top athletes in Trelawny. Lerone Clarke, who was in Usain's team for the 4x100 metres in Berlin, is from Trelawny, so is Veronica Campbell-Brown, the women's 200m champion in Beijing, while the Olympic sprinter Michael Green also went to William Knibb. But there has never been anyone quite like Usain.

He wanted to run every race in school for his house team. He did 100, 200, 400, 1500, the relays and even cross country, but didn't take training very seriously at first. We had to put pressure on him to make sure he went to training and called in his father, who thankfully made sure his son did as he was told. Usain wasn't a difficult child to deal with, but he just loved life. I'd describe him as playful, he couldn't sit still. He would be forever flicking the back of my ear and running off.

I wouldn't say he was completely dedicated to his school work, which is why Mrs Lee brought in Norman Peart to look after him. That was the making of Usain. Norman was a former pupil at William Knibb, who was an outstanding student and a good athlete. He understood the pressures on top young sportsmen when they were also trying to get an education. The idea was that Usain might go on to a scholarship at a US college, and to do that he not only had to be a good athlete but had to pass his exams too. As it turned out he never showed any interest in going to an American university.

When he first came to us he was also well known as a cricketer, but we wanted him for athletics. The cricket coach had to tell him, 'I'm sorry, I can't keep you.' Usain wanted to play fooball too, but we said he couldn't do that either. We were saying, 'Leave the football alone, man.' We told him he had a gold mine in his legs.

I would make sure he had all the training gear he needed, and since he won the world juniors we have never wanted for anything in terms of equipment because Puma supply it all.

We all went to the world juniors in Kingston, and while I thought Usain could win, I was so nervous I couldn't watch. His coach Mr Barnett had to tap me on the shoulder to tell me he'd done it. It was a great achievement for a 15-year-old to come out on top in a world event for those aged up to 19. It didn't matter to him when he was up against older boys, he liked the challenge.

I watched the Beijing 100 metres on a big screen in Falmouth, where an Olympic village had been set up for the townspeople. There was a wonderful atmosphere and I cried with joy. When he crossed that line, slowing down and looking around all over the place, it was exactly the same as he used to do it in school. The criticism aimed at him for the way he smiles and laughs in his races is unfair. That's how he always was. I've known Usain since he was 12, and that smile has never left his face. Even at that age he would turn round and call to his opponents to hurry up. You'd have needed a very long camera lens to get some of them in the picture. He wasn't being disrespectful to the other athletes, he was just out there enjoying himself.

The evening after he won the 100 metres I went to see his dad at his shop. He'd always supported the school in everything we did for Usain, and he was a very happy man. Parents deserve credit when their children do well. As a teacher I know how important they can be, and without his dad's influence, Usain might not have achieved what he has.

Usain tells people I'm his second mother and still calls me Miss T. I'm always in his corner and tell him, 'Win, lose or draw, whenever you go out there always do your best, because doing your best is good enough, and if you fall, I will be there for you.' We have not seen the best of Usain. I think he can go faster – if he takes it a bit more seriously.

CHAPTER 15
STRIVING
FOR
MORE

MY SEASON IDEALLY STARTS IN NOVEMBER, when I begin preparation for the year, which goes up to September in some cases. This really gives me six weeks' vacation, most of which is spent carrying out sponsorship duties. Six weeks is about the same amount as a business executive gets. So my job, although not nine to five, involves long hours of hard work.

Take a close look ... The scoliosis has forced my hips out of alignment which, as I said, makes my right leg shorter than my left. If you watch me closely you can see how I subconsciously push my weight on to my right side, because it feels awkward standing on my left leg and I have to bend my knee to balance. The problem caused a lot of hamstring pulls and is why it was once thought I should give up the sport. But we worked out that keeping my back strong was the key to avoiding injuries, and I do a lot of back exercises to keep myself supple. Even today sitting in the same position for too long causes my back to ache. It used to be agony in economy on a long-haul plane flight. I had to keep getting up to walk around, or I would have seized up. Travelling first class eases the pain.

I'm so lucky that I'm raw talent. If I really worked at it I could be extremely good indeed, but I never have. Yes, I put the effort in at times, but I could do more. I'm able to run 9.9 seconds in a competitive 100m race without any training at all. If I train right, eat right, go to the gym all the time and dedicate myself 100 per cent, then I definitely will do crazy times. At the moment I still don't do everything 100 per cent, missing gym and training sometimes, and not doing all my workouts. It's hard, man. I don't know how some sportsmen do it.

But coach will never let me neglect training completely. If he says we need to get things done, we get them done. He knows what I'm like, but I respect him enough to know that when he says it's time to work, then it is. Everything goes on hold, even parties. I've proved I can get serious; it's just doing it over a sustained length of time that is the difficulty.

" I'M SO LUCKY THAT I'M RAW TALENT. IF I REALLY WORKED AT IT I COULD BE EXTREMELY GOOD INDEED, BUT I NEVER HAVE "

When I'm in full swing, I get down to the Spartan Gym in Kingston in the morning and do a full one-hour workout which involves weights, bench presses, leg presses, tricep pull-downs, behind head pull-downs, arm curves, rowing, calf raises, leg extensions, special abs work and maybe a few squats – although not too many with my dodgy back, and definitely no treadmill because if I jog for too long my calf gets tight.

There are huge mirrors round the gym and if my muscles and abs are not sharp I don't like seeing my reflection. I tend to look more and

more once I start getting the abs right, although they'll never be as good as Merlene Ottey's. She was an iconic figure in Jamaican athletics, and when I saw her abs at the age of 44 they were a lot better than mine. 'Damn,' I thought, 'she's looking good.' Her abs were rock hard, and I might as well not have had any compared to her. It made me realise I needed to work out a lot more.

I confess to being body-conscious, and when I see my muscles standing out I know I'm working hard. You can tell you're in shape by looking at the muscle tone. I know how I'm supposed to look at a certain point of the year as I'm building up to the start of the season. When I've had a good month's training I can feel the benefits and see them.

After the gym workout I'll go home and maybe eat some pasta, reluctantly, and then it's off to training at about 4pm, when the sun is less intense. We go through the drills of the day which typically might consist of five 200m runs, or five 150m sprints, or a mixture of the two, one of which will be a proper competitive race with my club-mates, followed by various exercises and a visit to the massage table to ease my aching back.

Being 6ft 5ins tall with size 13 feet is, apparently, not good for a sprinter. I've been told that a study by the *Journal of Sports Science and Medicine* discovered that world champion sprinters have typically been between 5ft 9ins and 6ft 3ins. Admittedly, when you are my height and with those feet it takes time to get going but, then again, I make up the ground quicker because I've got a bigger stride than everyone else. When I won the 100m gold and set the world record in Berlin I covered the distance in 41 strides to Tyson Gay's 44, but my stride frequency was the same as his. I ran almost full out in that race. I was looking around a little bit, but not too much, and it's probably the hardest I've run. That might sound like a strange thing to say, but I set the world record the year before at the Olympics without running hard.

No one's been able to explain why I'm so fast. Maybe I'm a freak of nature, maybe scoliosis actually helps, I don't know. However I'm put together, though, it works.

My height did make starting a problem, but I've improved dramatically since working on the 100 metres with Glen Mills. I used to come up off the blocks too quickly, instead of completing my drive phase, which lost me vital time. The first four strides have got to be powerful and you have to stay low. Now I rise up gradually over about 35 metres. It's only at 50 metres that you should be completely upright.

Improving my time in the 200 metres has been about concentrating on the corner and negotiating it correctly. You can be the fastest man in the field and lose if you take the bend wrongly. I had to practise, practise, practise, practise and did so much work on it. I used to lean into the corner, but that's not the right way; you should do it the way a racing car driver goes into a corner. As you reach the apex you are going to go wide automatically, but you want to be sliding back across so that you stay in the middle of the lane. Any leaning should be slightly forward rather than to the side. Michael Johnson would run completely upright and at times seemed to be leaning backwards. It worked for him, but it never did for me; nor does it for the majority of sprinters.

RACING COMES EASILY TO ME, ESPECIALLY THE 100 METRES

I always looked up to Johnson as an athletics hero, because his was the era before mine. But Don Quarrie was the legend in Jamaica and my favourite athlete. I've seen tapes of some of Quarrie's races and he was like the best corner man ever, so smooth. It's a very specialised thing to be able to run a corner properly. That is why, no matter how fast I run the 100 metres, the 200 will always mean more to me, because of the effort I've put into it.

My reaction time to the gun has also got better. Training partners Daniel Bailey and Yohan Blake are very competitive on starts, and that has helped improve my reaction times. We have some great contests, and whoever does it best has bragging rights for a week. It's not easy to get it right. If you go a fraction of a second early, the pressure eases on the blocks and you will be called for a false start. You could also stumble at the gun, which is always a danger with my big feet, but you can't afford to worry about that, you have to stay focused on positives. If you let doubts creep in, it's trouble.

The first step after the gun is vital. You must make sure you are balanced on your centre of gravity, with the next steps being dictated by the first one. One of the basic mistakes of sprinters is to start off so fast that they shorten their stride and tip over. Making sure it's smooth and balanced is the most important thing.

The racing comes easily to me, especially the 100 metres. I don't have any great preparation routine. I might do some stride-outs and stretches and get a bit of a massage, but most of the time I'm just messing around. I used to listen to my iPod, but Coach banned it because he

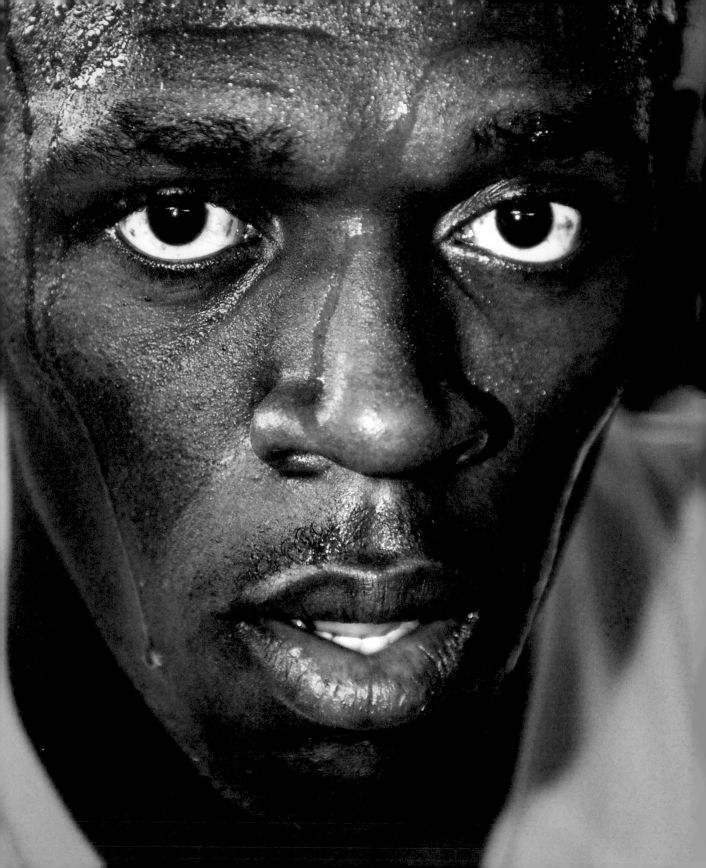

says it stops you concentrating properly. I don't worry about who I'm racing against or what's going to happen, I just go out there, entertain the crowd, and win. I don't need a psychologist or anyone to help my mind. I can work it out myself. I think my attitude has rubbed off on a lot of the other athletes, who aren't nearly as intense as they used to be, having seen that the laid-back approach works for me.

I will check out the crowd, wave to them, think about how I'm going to entertain them, do a bit for the camera when it focuses in on me, and make sure the spectators in the stadium and those watching on TV enjoy themselves.

It's not until the starter says 'Take your marks' that I'm properly focused on the race. I'm never nervous. I hardly think about it till I get down on the blocks.

I'd like to cut out the habit of looking around me as I run, because I know it would improve my times. It's a bad habit that I've had since high school, and I do wonder if Coach will carry out his threat to put blinkers on me. He has threatened to do it often enough.

When I get it all right by focusing better, sharpening up my start, staying low right through the drive phase, not looking around, and going flat out across the line, I'm going to be good, very good.

" I DON'T WORRY ABOUT WHO I'M RACING AGAINST OR WHAT'S GOING TO HAPPEN, I JUST GO OUT THERE, ENTERTAIN THE CROWD, AND WIN "

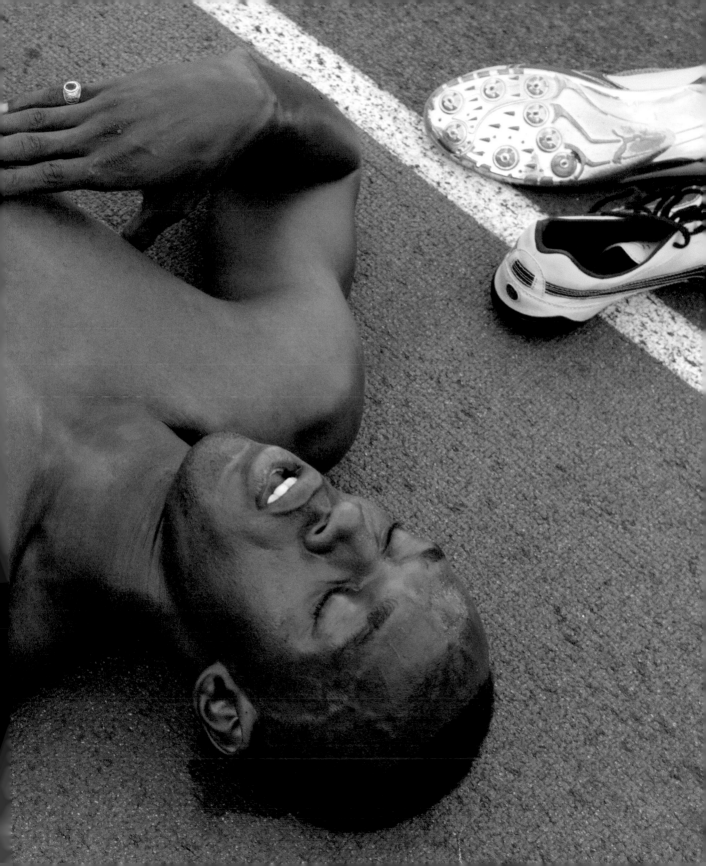

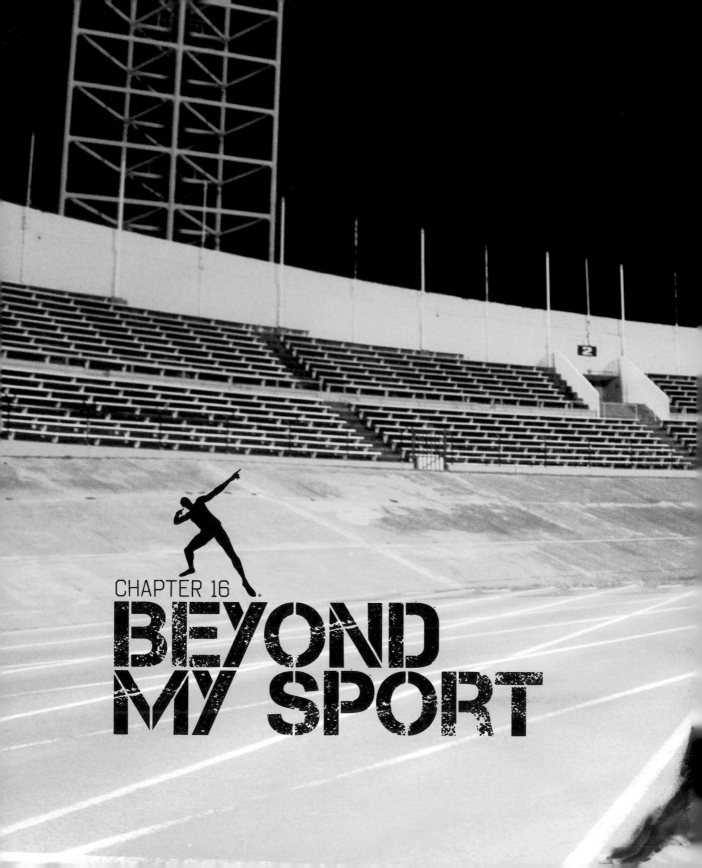

CHAPTER 16
BEYOND
MY SPORT

WHEN I'M FINISHED WITH ATHLETICS, I want to relax and maybe own a few businesses, but I would still play football every Sunday evening with my friends.

I am a great fan of football, and I especially admire Cristiano Ronaldo and Wayne Rooney. Not all the guys in the game are skilful, they've just got a turn and a good shot. I watch Emmanuel Adebayor, who plays for Manchester City, and think, 'I could do that.' I call him 'One-touch'. If you look at Adebayor's goals he uses his first touch to turn and beat you and then tries to kick it in the back of the net. I realise that sometimes if he takes more than one touch he loses the ball.

Ideally if I was to play football I'd sign for my favourite team Manchester United. People might say that's not realistic, but nobody's seen me play so you never know. If Alex Ferguson saw me in one of those charity matches he might think I could be the man to replace Ryan Giggs. Or maybe when Ferguson retires I might call up the new coach and say, 'Listen to me, Rooney needs somebody to support him now – I'll be that one.'

I was a lover of all sports when I was growing up. I took up athletics because I was the fastest, but I did enjoy playing cricket and football. If there was a big football match on TV, I'd be watching it, and sometimes I'd end up being late for training and as you can imagine my coach would give me an earful.

The Brazilian striker Ronaldo was the first footballer I remember admiring from watching games on television, then Juan Sebastian Veron and Gabriel Batistuta became my football heroes and Argentina my team. While most Jamaicans supported Brazil, I thought I'd be different and cheer on their big rivals. I had to make an exception at the 1998 World Cup, though, when the Reggae Boyz of Jamaica were in the finals. My own country had to come first that time, but we aren't in the World Cup very often so you need another team.

I used to go and watch Jamaica and got to know Ricardo Gardner, who is with the English Premier League team Bolton Wanderers, and Ricardo Fuller, who is also in England, playing centre-forward for Stoke City.

When we got to World Cup '98 we did it by skill, which is what we do well. I feel they are trying to change that and to make Jamaicans play like they do in England, even though that is not our natural way. In Walter Boyd and Theodore Whitmore we had skilful footballers who would take on five guys on the field and, if they lost it, no one minded – they had tried. That's what made them so interesting. Skills are what Jamaica is all about, and the team will only rise again when we get that philosophy back.

I started following Manchester United because of the Dutch striker Ruud Van Nistelrooy, a tremendous goalscorer who was always in the right place at the right time. After he left to go to Real Madrid, I kept supporting United because I enjoyed the way the team played.

While in Manchester for the 150m race before the 2009 World Championships, I was lucky enough to be invited to United's training ground, although I wasn't allowed to join in because they had an important game against Arsenal the next day. Alex Ferguson may regret missing the chance to see me in action.

I saw United draw the Arsenal game to win the Premier League title, and what a moment it was to be in the directors' box at Old Trafford! I had a video camera with me for both days and the tape is one of my most treasured possessions. There is a shot of Rooney, the England striker, who for a bit of fun was playing in goal during training, and when he made a good save he turned to me and said, 'Make sure you put that on YouTube.'

At the time there was a lot of media interest in me advising Cristiano Ronaldo – who became the FIFA World Player of the Year –

how to run properly. It's true I suggested a tip about putting his knee further forward to stop falling over when he runs at top speed, but I don't know if he was listening. After all, if you fall down it helps you get free-kicks and penalties and, when you've been running the same way as long as he has, it's hard to change. I know how difficult it is to alter your style as a sprinter, and that's without a ball at your feet.

My house is packed out with friends when United have a game on, not just with those who support the team like me, my brother and NJ, but also the 'Man United Haters Club', who come round to cheer anyone who is playing against us.

If we are against Arsenal, Chelsea, Liverpool or Manchester City, I get very worked up, and you will hear me start cussing when we miss chances. My hater friends love it, and we get into some right arguments in very fast Jamaican patois that would be incomprehensible to anyone else.

One of the best matches I ever saw was the 4–3 derby win against Man City last season and it almost got me into trouble with air traffic control. Oh my God, was that a game! I was supposed to be getting on a plane in Antigua but was watching in the VIP departure lounge and couldn't move.

They were calling me for the plane and my friends were saying, 'We've got to go, we've got to go, now,' but I said I wasn't leaving till the match was over. When it went into injury time they said the plane was going without me. I stayed where I was, and when Michael

I DON'T RESENT WHAT THE FOOTBALLERS EARN, YOU CAN'T DO THAT, BUT I THINK WE TRAIN HARDER THAN THEM.

Owen scored the winner it was fantastic. I was running around like one of the players and just made the plane thanks to a very understanding cabin crew. I may have enjoyed some special privileges that day. We took off late and my belated apologies to any of the passengers who were inconvenienced – United just seemed too important.

I saw Cristiano Ronaldo again after he joined Real Madrid. We'd done an interview at this big newspaper in Madrid and, as we left, I looked at his car and said, 'I like your Ferrari, nice.' You know what he replied? 'Yeah, but I need to get a new one because I don't like the colours.' I was thinking, 'Are you serious? It's a Ferrari and you are going to change it because you don't like the colours?' It was then I thought, wow, imagine if I had played professional football.

I don't resent what footballers earn, you can't do that, but I think we train harder than them. We are practising for seven months each season before we start running competitively, but then on the other hand they play so many games. We run maybe 20 times in a year, but they play 50 to 60 games for 90 minutes each time, so overall they probably do more work than us.

Real Madrid's Bernabeu Stadium was a spectacular place. The sound goes straight up and then comes crashing back down on you. I walked on the pitch to do a ceremonial kick-off and have never been so nervous in my life, with all the fans chanting my name. I only had to kick off but, man, I was shaking. It must be great for those guys to go out there each time with the crowd screaming for them. Maybe it's not so good if they're losing, though.

I didn't get to go out on the pitch at Old Trafford, but I have some great souvenirs of my day there. The goalkeeper Edwin Van der Sar gave me his jersey from the match against Arsenal, and I bought all the other players' shirts, which I have hanging in my walk-in wardrobe at home. I've also got shirts of Kaka's, Van Nistelrooy's and Raul's, and, though I'm a United fan, I'm proud to own a signed England shirt from the Liverpool captain Steven Gerrard, which he wore in a friendly against Egypt.

There is another souvenir from my encounters with footballers which astonishes me even now. It came from Samuel Eto'o, who used to play for Barcelona. We were doing an event for *L'Equipe*, the French sports paper, and I was looking at his watch, which had so many diamonds round it, I was almost blinded. He saw me looking and said, 'Do you like the watch?' I replied, 'Yeah, it's good.' He took it off and handed it to me saying, 'You can have it.' I was left standing with my mouth open holding this watch, which was so heavy it felt like it would break my arm. I just about managed a thank you and he said 'No problem' and walked off. I don't wear the watch too often because it's so heavy, but I still have it on the dressing table in my bedroom. I found out it's worth 35,000 euros.

I've bridged a sporting divide between athletics and football. Diehard football fans know who I am, which is great. They go, 'Hey, Usain Bolt, you're the man,' and I have to sign a ton of autographs, but it's good, awesome.

I'm constantly amazed how if I go to a football dinner, everyone wants my signature and to have a photograph with me.

And it shocks me how a lot of players know me. I met the Chelsea star Didier Drogba in a club in London and he was like 'Usain Bolt!!!!' I thought it should have been the other way round, with me wanting to see him, because when it comes to strikers he's one of the best goalscorers in the world. He's so strong and skilful and so often in the right place at the right time, it's like he can see into the future. He gave me his number but I lost it along with Frank Lampard's and Ronaldo's too. Sorry for not ringing, guys.

My favourite sports are soccer, basketball and cricket, and I will watch a bit of tennis if the Williams sisters are playing or Roger Federer. I like car rallying too, but I'm not so much into Nascar or Formula One grand prix racing, which is too long. No one ever seems to overtake and the only excitement is when they go into the pits.

My basketball team is the Boston Celtics, and I support them because of one man, Kevin Garnett, who won a gold medal at the

" CHRIS GAYLE CAN RACE ME OVER 100 METRES ANYTIME HE WANTS... "

2000 Olympics. Garnett is a very good role model to me, he's very determined and puts his heart and soul into everything he does. When he's injured, or sitting on the bench, he is still cheering his team on, and that's a good example for any sportsman. When he's not out there on the court he's like another coach. I met Kevin when we did the Gatorade commercial together for the Superbowl, and I really look up to him – which even I have to do because he is 7ft tall.

I watch quite a bit of basketball. Most games are on in Jamaica at around 8pm at night, and I get quite excitable when the Celtics are playing, just like I do with United. At primary school I always thought I'd be a cricketer, and I think that's what my dad wanted. He was a real cricket fan. Pakistani Waqar Younis was one of the best bowlers ever, and his in-swinging yorker was like nothing else I've ever seen.

The fact that in high school they wouldn't let cricket interfere with my athletics curbed my interest, which waned further with the decline of the West Indies as a team.

I'm not a big watcher of Test matches unless the West Indies captain Chris Gayle is batting – when he gets out, I leave. Test cricket can be boring unless the batsmen are trying to score runs. I'm not into the science of it, I'm an aggressive type. I like the way the Australians Matthew Hayden and Adam Gilchrist play, as well as the English guys Kevin Pietersen and Andrew Flintoff, and the Indian Virender Sehwag. Like Gayle, they play an aggressive, entertaining game.

Test cricket is better than it used to be, though. Years ago the emphasis was on not getting out and playing no shots at all, with the aim of getting a draw. Every ball outside off stump the batsman would leave. At least now teams try to win rather than making the draw their first objective.

Gayle has become a good friend of mine and I like to give him advice about his game – although, like Ronaldo, I'm not sure that he listens. I am forever telling him to leave the running to me, because he is always

running himself out. I think he still hasn't listened to me. Bowling Gayle in a charity cricket match is one of my treasured moments. Honestly, it was right up there with winning the Olympics.

There was a big crowd in and it was an awesome day. We'd been at each other's neck beforehand, having met in a club where I was saying, 'I'm going to get you,' and we were generally mugging each other off. He said, 'You'll never get me out,' and that in any case he had bribed the umpire to call a no-ball against me if I did hit his stumps, just to make sure. Well, he didn't bribe the umpire enough.

The game involved pro cricketers and invited guests, and I swear I psyched Chris out. I knew he would be trying to pull me and was going to go after anything too close to his body, so you had got to keep it outside off stump. I sent the ball down, he went to whack it and it came off the inside edge of his bat and shattered his stumps to give me my prize wicket.

But I'm a fair man. Having proved I can bowl him out, I'm going to let him try and get his revenge and even things up. He can race me over 100 metres any time he wants.

JENNIFER BOLT

MOTHER

From the day he started school, Usain would run all the way there. He was way faster than the other kids, although at that age you don't think of your child as a future Olympic sprinter, you just wonder how you're going to keep up with him.

He was seven when he won his first cup for running. I watched the race and he won easily, going further and further away from the others. He was enjoying life and making the most of it, and the teachers told me what a talented sportsman he was.

Usain was a good boy, curious and full of fun too, always joking and messing with me. Even today he will sit on my lap when he comes home and calls me 'Mummy'. He will always be my little boy and I'm still way too soft with him. When I go to his house in Kingston it's just like when he lived at home. I get on with the washing and the cooking as if we were back in Trelawny.

We never called him by his proper name of Usain but by his pet name of VJ, in keeping with the Jamaican tradition that everyone has a pet name. Mine is Jen-Jen, which is a bit more explainable than VJ. I can't remember why we came up with that, there was no particular reason for it. His dad, Wellesley, is known as Gideon, and no one knows why that is either. I always call him Gideon, never Wellesley.

Usain would sometimes go to church with me at the weekends but usually a lot later than I did. You have to be at church by nine, and he would be lurking around or lying in bed and wouldn't come until nearly eleven, when church finished. I'm quite religious, and he has some beliefs, but he's not a big churchgoer. He preferred spending time with his video games and watching the cartoons on TV.

We would always have breakfast and dinner together as a family. He loved bacon and eggs for breakfast and dumplings too. As long as it wasn't fish he was happy.

When he came home from school he would do his homework then be out playing with his little group of friends, but only as far as the gate, where I could see him. He was forever running around. You would see him one minute and the next he was gone. I never knew he could be one of the greatest runners until he won the world juniors. The evening before he went off to Kingston for the race he cried because he didn't want to go. He said, 'All the other runners are bigger than me.' He was 15 and some of the others were nearly 18. We had to sit down and talk to him with his grandmother before we got him to go.

I went to Beijing for the Olympics and had butterflies in my stomach for the 100

metres but I was determined to watch. I sat quietly till the end of the race and then went wild. Norman Peart was beside me telling me it was a world record, and I thought, 'That's my boy.' I was so proud. I'm not an emotional person really, but it was so exciting and I gave him a hug. I was much more relaxed for the 200 metres, I knew he'd win.

Sometimes his life now scares me. He is out and about in a land where there are a lot of incidents of crime and violence. I'm not fearful because he is famous, I'm just acting like any mother. He likes clubbing, but I went out too, so I know what it's like and what dangers there are. I tell him to be careful because not everyone around him has good intentions.

He has changed my life and all our lives, but we have got used to it. We live the way we always have, we are simple people. We are very close, and any mother would be proud of him. Everybody tells me I have a wonderful child and that they wish he was their son.

CHAPTER 17

THE FUTURE

THERE IS ONE PROMISE I CAN MAKE about the future – the 2016 Olympics in Brazil will be my last major competition. I won't be the type of athlete who obstinately keeps on going in a vain attempt to defy the passage of time. I want to be a legend in the sport, and that means defending my titles from 2008 at the London Olympics in 2012, but I want to go out at the top, when I'm still unbeatable.

I am not a legend yet. Anyone can win an Olympics. Winning once is not the mark of a great athlete, in my estimation; you have to do it again if you are to stand out from the crowd. Michael Johnson took four gold medals in three successive Olympics and eight golds in four World Championships, which definitely makes him a legend. So too was Ed Moses, the 400m hurdler, who was first in 122 consecutive races, won gold in the Olympics of 1976 and 1984, and didn't lose for nearly ten years between August 1977 and June 1987.

In Don Quarrie's case I will break my own rule about what qualifies you as a legend, because although he failed to defend his 200m title at the Moscow Olympics he still got a bronze, and then took a silver in the relay at the 1984 Games in Los Angeles. Quarrie is a national sporting hero and a man all Jamaican athletes admire, although the daddy of them all was Arthur Wint, who won Jamaica's first ever gold medal over 400 metres in 1948 and then the 4x400 metres in 1952. He also won silvers in both Games at 800 metres.

When I met Johnson I asked what persuaded him to retire after he turned 33, and he told me there was nothing else to do. He had broken world records, defended titles at the Olympics and World Championships, gone on winning streaks and beaten everybody. He was bored and there was no reason to go on.

I don't think I'll get bored. What will make me finish is knowing how hard you've got to train to achieve the same things over again. If I didn't have to train I'd probably go on for ever, because I enjoy the whole camaraderie of an event, the travelling, being with my friends and the competition.

I might do the 400 metres and the long jump at the Brazil Olympics, which finishes on my 30th birthday, and then have one more season on the circuit after that before calling it a day in 2017. I've been asked why I don't try the World Indoor Championships for a change, but it's not for me. In the 200 metres the bends are too tight, and I think I would seriously hurt myself if I tried the 60 metres because I wouldn't be able to stop in time. I'm a big guy and when I get going at full speed off those blocks it takes time to slow down. There's not enough run-off space in the 60 metres before you go crashing into the foam mattresses at the end. I know they're only soft, but I'd still be hitting them fairly hard and would be tempted to pull up a bit, which could cause an injury.

I won't be running beyond the age of 32, no matter what. You could offer me 50 million dollars and I wouldn't do it. Some people go on running until they cannot physically put one leg in front of the other, but that won't be me.

Merlene Ottey, who raced for Jamaica with such distinction for so many years, wanted to go on for ever. After falling out with the Jamaican team over her selection for the Sydney Games she changed nationalities and went on to compete for her new nation, Slovenia, in Athens at the age of 44. She very nearly made it to Beijing in 2008, but just failed to qualify. I think Merlene was trying to set the record for the person who kept doing track and field the longest. She should have retired and left us with memories only of her as a brilliant sprinter, because she was really, really good. I've met her a few times and she's cool – and man, those abs!

I want to get married some day, but that will be after I retire from track and field, definitely not before. I'll take my time to meet the right girl, I don't want to rush into anything. Right now I'm too busy with my career and enjoying life to settle down. I do want children soon, though, some time after the next Olympics.

I'll be strict as a dad too, because it was how I was brought up. I will have my own way of doing it, and I don't think I'll be as strict keeping my children in check, the way Dad did with me. I watched and took note, and I saw where my dad went wrong and how he lost direction a little bit. He stifled me by not letting me go out much and treated my sister the same way. He didn't give us any free space.

My children will have more freedom, but I'll expect them to be good at school. It's all about trust and knowing your kid will do the right thing. I knew this girl at William Knibb who went to parties from the age of 15, and her dad had no problem with her going because he trusted her. He explained life to her, about how guys are, and she never had a boyfriend even by the time she was 18 – and she had plenty of offers – because she felt she was not ready for one. She was allowed to go anywhere. Her dad knew she wasn't going to do anything wrong, and that's the way to go.

If I had a daughter I wouldn't be extra strict, because if a father behaves like that, he can lose her. I've seen it happen with my sister. Your daughter will start to sneak around and do all kinds of crazy stuff.

If my first child is a boy, though, I'm going to warn him about track and field and how very hard it will be for him. I don't just mean the training required. Can you imagine the pressure he will be under as the son of Usain Bolt? From the moment he can stand on his own two feet he will be expected to run to the shop quicker than anyone else in the village. I'd prefer him to play a different sport. Maybe that is when the Bolt name will feature in football.

I don't see myself as an athletics coach. I couldn't do that, I don't have the patience. Some of the young athletes just do what they want and don't listen. If you have your own family you don't have the time to be stressed by those big guys as they grow up.

No, I want to be able to pick and choose what I do when I retire. I'm going to build a massive house in the country with a huge bedroom which has a rotating bed in it and a sliding window to take in the sunset. I saw it on the Snoop Dog and Pharrell music video 'Beautiful' and thought, 'Oh my God, that is beautiful.' The house will have lots of land, with a basketball court and a football pitch, and I'm going to build a course for quad biking. I realise that at this stage of my athletics career quad biking would not be the wisest thing to do. If I even mention it to the people who look after me they go, 'What! You can't do that.'

It's like the whole of Jamaica is telling me not to do anything dangerous. I went to a showroom to ask about buying an ordinary motorbike, and the salesman, who wasn't looking at me at the time, quoted a price. Then,

when he raised his head and saw who it was, he said, 'You're not getting a bike.' He was happy to do himself out of a sale rather than have me put my athletics career in jeopardy.

I don't have any insurance against my career being ended. My management looked into it, but I told them not to bother, it was so ridiculously expensive. I decided we should invest what the premiums would have been and get on with life. I don't think I'll ever be short of money whatever happens.

I don't know exactly what I'll do when I retire. Leave it to me to find something very interesting. Whatever it is, it will doubtless attract a lot of attention. My life has been a fascinating journey already. Let's see what happens next.

"MY LIFE HAS BEEN A FASCINATING JOURNEY ALREADY. LET'S SEE WHAT HAPPENS NEXT"

WELLESLEY (GIDEON) BOLT

FATHER

When Usain was six weeks old, he fell off the bed. I'd left him there, not realising he could push himself off, and it was the first indication of how active he was. He would never be still and I thought something was wrong with him, which is why I took him to see the doctor. The doctor said he was a hyperactive child who needed to use his energy up but was otherwise fine, and I would have to get used to it.

My early memories of him in sport are as a cricketer. I'm keen on cricket and could see Usain was a good batsman and bowler, but at the age of 12 we had to make a decision about whether he could continue playing or should concentrate on his running. After talking to the teacher it was decided cricket had to go.

I never dreamed Usain would get to the level he is now, but you could see he had a lot of ability. If William Knibb was prepared to award him a sports scholarship he had to have something going for him. His mother and I used to run 200 and 400 metres at primary school, so I suppose he must have got some ability from both of us. Maybe it was just the right combination. It annoyed me, though, when he didn't dedicate himself to training, and I had to be very strict with him about it.

He knew what was right and wrong and what would happen if he didn't do what he was told.

His mother and I had a good relationship with Usain, it was a happy home. Sometimes we would all sit together and play cards and dominoes, and he's never lost his love of dominoes. When it was time for study he had to go off with his books. Even when we knew he had a special talent as an athlete I would say, 'Your education comes first. Anything can happen to you on the track, but if you haven't got anything in the head then there is nothing that can come out to help you.'

I went to as many of his track meetings as I could when he was growing up. He raced at the Junior CARIFTA games in 2001, when he was 14, and did well, but that was only against other Caribbean countries. When he won the world juniors that was much bigger, and he won the Rising Star Award for 2002 and 2003.

That was his first really big race. I remember watching from the end of the stadium and how he had to work really hard down the straight to win, but he had the determination to do it. The race was on television too, and people across Jamaica got to know the name of Usain Bolt. They would come and congratulate me on his performances, but I wasn't taking it for granted that he could step up to senior competition.

There have been plenty of junior stars who have never made it, and his development was halted because of injuries caused by his back problem. That was a worrying time and I think it would have been better if he'd missed the Athens Olympics.

With Mr Mills as his coach things improved, and you could tell Usain was confident again. I heard a newsflash on the radio when he broke the world 100m record in New York and I was like 'What?' I felt bumps all over, I couldn't believe it. Then Usain rang to tell me all about it, and we had a laugh because I'd told him not to run in it. I thought 100 metres was just for fun and he should be doing the 200 and the 400.

I didn't go to Beijing at first. I don't like long flights. Then, when he won the 100 metres, his sponsors Digicel persuaded me to go. I had to fly to Los Angles and on to China, and in total it took 19 and a half hours. I found the whole experience a little scary. Though I missed the 200 metres as well, I was there when he won the relay. I enjoyed the party afterwards too, I was mobbed and was signing autographs, which was an unusual experience, I'd never done that before. The police had to pull people off me. I looked at Usain and thought, 'Really, this is my son?' How can a father not be proud?

I went to the World Championships, which was another long flight, and I almost lost my voice shouting during Usain's races. It's a wonderful thing for a dad to see his son break two world records. He's so relaxed when he's

running, you wonder how fast he can go.

It's all so far removed from our quiet existence in the country where I've spent all my life and where Usain grew up.

I used to work for a company called The Coffee Industry Tourist Board as an extension officer, advising farmers how to grow the beans, then checking whether they needed fertiliser or what kind of spray was required to treat diseased plants. I worked there for 16 years until I was made redundant just as Usain finished high school. Then with the redundancy money and a little help from Usain I opened a grocery store, selling meat products like cow's feet and dried goods.

I work at the shop seven days a week, on weekdays from nine till six and on Sundays from seven till noon. I'm always there, it's just me. I don't work with anyone else. The shop keeps me in the heart of the community, and the people who come in are friends I've known for years.

After Usain won the World Championships I don't think two days would pass without somebody visiting from another country. There were people from Belgium, Sweden, China, everywhere, wanting to see where he grew up, where he went to school, where I worked, everything. I woke up one morning at 6.30am and there were cars full of Germans who wanted to meet us. We've done so many interviews I've lost count. I don't mind and, as Usain says, 'Daddy, it's just part of it, so you have to do it.'

When you are in Europe and you see the attention he gets, it's crazy. I don't know how he deals with it. Like his running, he takes everything in his stride.

9.58

ACKNOWLEDGEMENTS

9.58 — MY STORY is my way of giving you an inside view of what my life has been like so far. It is cool to be the fastest man on earth, but there are lots of responsibilities with that title. I know my life will never be the same again.

I would like to say thanks to a number of people, but I will get in trouble if I start calling names. A lot of them are mentioned in the book anyway. But, for each of you who have played a meaningful role in helping me to become who I am today – and you definitely know who you are – I am eternally grateful.

I would like to use this opportunity to mention my family who has been there with me through thick and thin. I was lucky to have Mom and Dad as a unit and that helped tremendously. I would also like to highlight the role all my schools played in my life so far and to all the teachers who influenced me in a positive way. To my best friend, NJ, and now personal assistant – he knows me inside out. I would like to acknowledge my management team also.

My current coach Glen Mills and I have a special relationship and since 2004 he has helped me develop technically. He tells me we still have a lot of work to do. To my training partners at Racers Track Club, Jamaica, thanks for your input too.

I would also like to thank the team of readers, NJ and Carole Beckford, along with the team at HarperCollins who made sure this book was published really well.

From my community in Trelawny to the fast-paced city of Kingston, Jamaica and to the world, I have met thousands of people and each kind word from you means a lot to me.

Media has changed so much since I became a junior champion in 2002 and I would like to show appreciation for the support; social media – Facebook and Twitter are just phenomenal. Thanks for all your support.

Hard work, dedication and talent are three factors to my success so far, but I would like to give thanks to GOD for taking me thus far.

My journey continues ...

PHOTO CREDITS